Acknowledgments

My gratitude to the monks--Alex, Ann, Caverly, Dave, Deb, Jen, John, Melinda, Rich, Tom--for practicing so diligently the process described in this book.

Thank you to all who participated in the email classes, workshops, and retreats that provided the student-guide exchanges recounted here.

WHEN YOU'RE FALLING, DIVE

ACCEPTANCE, FREEDOM AND POSSIBILITY

CHERI HUBER

Also by Cheri Huber

From Keep It Simple Books
The Key and the Name of the Key Is Willingness*
How You Do Anything Is How You Do Everything: A Workbook
There Is Nothing Wrong With You: Going Beyond Self-Hate*
The Depression Book: Depression as an Opportunity for Spiritual Growth
The Fear Book: Facing Fear Once and for All*
Nothing Happens Next: Responses to Questions about Meditation
Be the Person You Want to Find: Relationship and Self-Discovery*
Sex and Money...are dirty, aren't they? A Guided Journal
Suffering Is Optional: Three Keys to Freedom and Joy

From A Center for the Practice of Zen Buddhist Meditation
That Which You Are Seeking Is Causing You to Seek
Time-Out for Parents: A Compassionate Approach to Parenting*
The Monastery Cookbook: Stories and Recipes from A Zen Kitchen

From Present Perfect Books (Sara Jenkins, editor)
Trying to Be Human: Zen Talks from Cheri Huber*
Turning Toward Happiness: Conversations with a Zen Teacher and Her Students
Good Life: A Zen Precepts Retreat with Cheri Huber
Buddha Facing the Wall: Interviews with American Zen Monks
Sweet Zen: Dharma Talks with Cheri Huber

*Videotapes from Openings***
There Are No Secrets: Zen Meditation with Cheri Huber
Yoga for Meditators *with Christa Rypins*
Yoga for A Better Back *with Christa Rypins and Dr. John Sousa*
Yummy Yoga: Stress Relief for Hips, Back, and Neck *with Christa Rypins*

*Audiotape from Who's Here? Productions***
Getting Started Going Deeper: Introduction to Meditation

*Available as a book on tape from Keep It Simple
**Also available from Keep It Simple
Please see the order form at the end of this book.
All items except books on tape are available through your local bookstore.

Cover design by Mary Denkinger
Cover art by Alex Mill
Photograph of Cheri Huber by Jane Lidz

Preface

Part of what I do as a Zen student and teacher is recognize blocks and hindrances that litter the path of awakening: unwillingness, intellectualizing, self-hate, resistance, as examples. Suddenly I will see one of those blocks everywhere and think, yes, this is it, I'll offer this to those who ask for guidance, and they will see and their suffering will end.

Results are mixed. Some are inspired by my latest "jag," while others don't find them quite as enlightening.

This is good. I enjoy it. It freshens the practice. It provides new metaphors, new mirrors, for the joyful and difficult work of seeing and letting go the causes of suffering.

Acceptance, the subject of this book, is and isn't one of my jags. It is in the sense that it has been the focus of my teaching for a while now; it isn't in the sense that acceptance is fundamental. Without acceptance all effort to awaken and end suffering rests on shaky ground.

When *You're Falling, Dive* illustrates how this is so, but to comprehend acceptance as I mean it requires you the reader to be open to a new understanding. An aspect of the Buddha's Eight-Fold Path for ending suffering, as we recite it at the Zen Monastery Practice Center, is "Compassionate comprehension the dissipates delusion."

In this spirit, I ask you to let go all notions of what acceptance means and be open to a new and, I trust, deeper and more compassionate understanding. To be rather blunt about it--and, really, why not?--you have nothing to lose except a lifetime of suffering.

In loving kindness,
Cheri

From the Author to the Reader

When speaking and writing, I use the following
terms interchangeably:
Egocentric karmic conditioning
Conditioned mind
Conditioning
Ego
Identity
Ego identity
Egocentricity
Illusion of separation
Illusion of a separate self

Each term points at the experience of feeling
oneself to be separate from life, separate
from the present moment, (in Christian
language) separate from God. Loneliness,
fear, desperation, disconnection, deprivation,
inadequacy, greed, hate and confusion are
common ways the illusion of being a separate
self manifests.

When You're Falling, Dive is another effort
to illustrate the practice of seeing through

that illusion and claiming the joy, compassion, clarity, and peace that is our birthright. I tend to switch back and forth between terms so if you're reading along and you're not sure you follow my point, please refer back to this page for a refresher.

Table of Contents

Preface
From the Author to the Reader

Part One: What Acceptance Is and Why We Resist

Part Two: How to Accept

Part Three: Acceptance, Freedom, and Possibility

PART ONE

What Acceptance Is and Why We Resist

What Is Acceptance?

Acceptance as I use it is different from our usual associations with the word. Acceptance is often thought of as what "losers" are left with.

"I've run out of options.
I can't make things work.
I guess I just have to accept failure and get on with my life."

The acceptance I'm talking about is not failure, defeat, resignation, giving up, or a last resort. Also, my use of the word acceptance does not necessarily imply agreement or condoning.

By acceptance I mean embracing, owning, and expanding beyond one's closely held and defended personal limitations. It is an attitude of "If it exists in my world, it is mine." It contains not only that which one believes one knows, but also that which has yet to be discovered. It is the deconstructing of one's illusions of understanding such that one is left with possibilities previously unimagined.

Acceptance is nothing less
than the complete transformation
of what one has believed to be one's self
and one's reality.

When we accept in this way--not defeated, not resigned, but triumphantly open and willing--we gain a larger perspective on ourselves and, thus, on life, for our lives are a projection of who we are. We accept that we are not separate from anything. We realize that resisting, hating, avoiding, and denying maintain that which we resist, hate, avoid, and deny. We accept that the only possibility for effecting the changes we so deeply desire is to move into the present with the willingness to see and embrace all that arises. Anything short of complete moment-by-moment acceptance of life exactly as it is, is resistance, and resistance leads invariably to suffering.

Through accepting responsibility for our lives,
we make peace with all that is not
as we would wish it to be.

It's not that we gain the power
to change circumstances;
we develop the skill to determine
our experience of those circumstances.

This is what the Buddha talked about as
ending suffering.

Turning the Fall into a Dive

Imagine this: you find yourself falling through midair, terrified, kicking and clawing and shrieking in a desperate attempt to stop the fall. Then something happens, a shift in perception, and you see it differently. Instead of resisting the fall, you let go, straighten out, align your body, head in the direction you're going anyway, and enjoy the ride.

"Great," you say, "if you're headed toward something soft, but..." This may not be the perfect metaphor, but to stick with it for the moment, I can assure you that the dive leads to what our hearts most long for, though we're usually too afraid to accept it. At the bottom of that dive is a pool of deep, clear, water: the freedom we all seek.

"Well, it's one thing for you to say there's a pool of water below, but if I can't see it, how can I be expected to just

LET GO?"

It's true that you cannot see the freedom that awaits you as long as you're flailing around, resisting what's happening. Even if (to continue the metaphor) you manage to catch onto a tree part-way through your fall, you still can't know what would happen if you let go, because all your attention is focused on clinging to the tree. You're still stuck in suffering.

"When you're falling, dive" means when you're resisting life, allow it to be what it is and the suffering will be over. The way we learn acceptance is through awareness. Through simple awareness, we can begin to free ourselves from the resistance, dissatisfaction, and fear that rob us of lives of ease and joy. To see how this works, we will undertake a self-examination, observing the effects of resistance in our lives and seeing how it keeps us stuck in suffering.

Why We Resist

It is a waste of time and energy to resist what is. Then why do we spend our lives in resistance? Because resistance maintains our sense of who we are by saying "no" to everything that doesn't support our identity.

Identity is maintained by repetitious thoughts spoken by authoritarian voices telling endless stories about who we are and then judging us for not measuring up to some ill-defined standard.

Identity is maintained by holding the body in particular configurations that produce emotional states that reinforce resistance. Examples: clenched jaw, tensed shoulders

Identity is maintained by never examining the belief that "IF I FEEL THIS, I MUST DO THAT."

The message is that resistance is necessary because life is threatening.

When resistance fails to produce the desired changes in our lives, we rarely let go, move into the present, and see other possibilities. We tighten more, tense harder, and attempt to control more completely.

But resistance does not lead to change.

Acceptance leads to change.

Letting Go of Resistance

The quickest way to let go of

RESISTANCE

is to let go of

the patterns

that maintain it.

STOP

repeating the same old
thoughts and stories and behaviors.

STOP

believing the voices
(in your head)
that tell you
how you are,
how others are,
how life is,

and just

WHY

you have to be
tight,
tense,
frightened,
small,
and controlled.

IT'S ALL A BIG LIE!

None of it is true.
It never has been.
it never will be.

What Is Required

Stopping those patterns
requires acceptance.

ACCEPT

...that what we see is something that is
programmed in us, rather than the only
reality.

...that we may have opinions about what's
going on, but in fact we have not deeply
examined life and don't really know.

...that all that has brought us to this point
has happened and is the way it is.

...that what we've been taught to believe
may not be true.

...that we cannot make life or ourselves be
the way we've been taught to think they
should be.

...that our emotions, while maintaining a particular view of life, will never get us anywhere but stuck.

...that being angry, feeling victimized, and hating ourselves will never give us the lives we want.

...that this is what is. This is who I am right now, and this is what I've got.

...that we hate being required to accept what is, that life is not as we would have it be.

...that we are angry and afraid.

We are required to accept even the parts of ourselves who don't want to accept.

All of life comes down to
this moment,
right here,
right now,
either resisting or accepting.

SUFFERING or FREEDOM

Choose.

When we don't accept what is, when we dig in
our heels and say no to life, what are we
doing? Are we holding evil at bay?
Are we ending injustice?
Are we making the world a safer place?
Or are we just maintaining our own ego
identity? Are we simply being "right,"
justifying our opinions and beliefs, and keeping
our own little reality intact?

I cannot imagine a situation in life that would
not be made clearer by letting go of
programmed beliefs and assumptions and
allowing a deeper wisdom than conditioned
opinions to guide us to what might be
beneficial in each situation.

Here's the good news.

If I'm mistaken about this--if, after
accepting,
     opening,
          letting go,
               being in the present
               moment with life as it is,

we find that being
tight,
     tense,
          frightened,
               small,
                    and controlled

actually IS the fast track to ending suffering,
to happiness, to having the lives we want, we
can always tense up again, repeat our
familiar stories, work up our emotions, and
get back to our previous program.

What's Wrong?

When we catch ourselves thinking about what's wrong, it's good to ask, what does "wrong" mean? How do we know when something is wrong? In considering this question we can uncover many unconscious aspects of what wrong means for us.

If we look closely enough, we will see that wrong almost always boils down to something we personally don't like, don't approve of, don't want, or to something we fear or envy. But can we go beyond individual judgments to find a universal wrong? Greed, war, hatred, torture-- all of us might oppose those, and yet it's not hard to see how we all regularly participate in and benefit from them. Even with child abuse, we must acknowledge our passive complicity through titillating advertising, show business, and "news" stories, along with our lack of concern about the living conditions of children in poverty, the effects of racism and discrimination, the fate of children left to fend for themselves when parents are jailed on minor drug charges, children who are forced to sell their bodies to survive, those without health care, and so on.

But let's agree that child abuse is wrong. Does that mean it shouldn't happen? It does happen. Does it mean we should hate and punish the people who do it? What about those who allow it, all of us, in our apathy and self-centeredness? Or are we saying the only one to be hated and punished is the one who directly hits, humiliates, violates, has sex with, or otherwise harms the child?

If we agree that only the person who directly hurts the child should be punished--that our hands are clean--what do we do now? First we must judge. Judgment is our best proof we are different from the abuser. "I am not like that. I can see what that person is doing and know that it is wrong. I am therefore in a position to judge."

Now what?

Next, we must decide on the punishment. Keep in mind we are not applying any of the excuses, explanations, rationalizations, or slippery thinking we allow ourselves under similar circumstances. It doesn't matter where this person comes from or what has created him or her, once a person has done wrong, the only possibility is punishment.

Why?

Is it our experience that punishment works?

Has punishing wrongdoers ended wrongdoing?

Have we devised any punishment that has had a substantial effect on wrongdoing?

No, not really.

Yet we remain convinced that punishment is necessary. We must judge and punish or society will suffer from

crime, abuse, dishonesty, and victimization.

Of course we currently judge and punish, and always have, and society still suffers from

crime, abuse, dishonesty, and victimization.

Might we seek another possibility?

Our Problems

What if we all took on "what's wrong" in the world as our personal responsibility? Instead of trying to find out who is at fault, whom we should blame, what if we acknowledged all our societal ills as "our problems"?

What might be possible?

Imagine leaders of two countries coming together to work for peace. What if they saw the conflicts of their two nations as "our problem"? Let's say you and I are those two leaders. You have people in your country who want peace and those who want conflict. I have people in my country who want peace and those who want conflict. That's OUR problem. So, when people who want conflict act out in a way designed to stall the peace process neither of us says, "No more peace talks until you get control of your people." Instead we both acknowledge this viewpoint and behavior in our populations, agree that it is a problem, and work together toward a resolution. Of course there is history between our people--a hateful, angry, violent history. Of course people get upset, disagree, feel frustrated, feel like victims, want to retaliate--THAT'S OUR PROBLEM. If our citizens didn't feel this way, we would have peace already. Our task is to accept the whole of our situation and work to reach the place that is most compassionate to all.

Is this pie-in-the-sky, Pollyanna-ish twaddle that has no place in the "real" world?

Of course not. Mahatma Gandhi won independence for India using this approach.

Anything is possible, but we must accept the possibility.

Our first task is to accept that something other than the way it's always been is available to us.

Counseling couples offers an illuminating
scenario. The partners enter the room,
sit on opposite sides facing each other,
plop their problems down in the center,

and begin pointing blaming fingers at one
another across the problems. The first task
is to bring the couple together, sitting side by
side, looking at "our problem." This is
essential: no lasting solution will be found until
problems becomes "our problems."

What might this look like on an individual
level? We have all
the same conflicts
inside ourselves
that we encounter
outside ourselves.
In fact, I contend
that there is no

"outside"--that all the problems we perceive
outside ourselves exist because we project
our internal workings "out there." Conflict
within ourselves, with one other person, in a
community, and between nations is exactly the
same process.

We have spent the entire history of
humankind attempting to solve problems "out
there" that can only be resolved "in here."

Let's say you want to accomplish a certain thing. You set out in the direction of accomplishment. However, not all the aspects of yourself want you to accomplish this goal. There are parts of you who don't want you to change, who feel threatened, who have their identity in your failure. This is your problem.

Your problem is not the fact that you're inherently flawed and that there's something wrong with you, though that's what we have all been taught to believe about ourselves. Trying and failing is not proof that you are inadequate, wrong, and doomed to failure. It is proof that you are a "mini-world," with all the fear, hatred, conflict, ideals, hurts, and dreams of the larger world. As you prove this to yourself, it will be obvious that our greatest opportunity as human beings is first to resolve these conflicts in ourselves and then to work together to resolve them for all.

How? Step by step, through acceptance. You draw a circle of acceptance and begin to work systematically with the part of you who keeps a particular piece of content outside the circle of acceptance.

STEP 1

You recognize where you hold that resistance in your body.

STEP 2

You listen to the voices in your head about why this particular thing is unacceptable.

STEP 3

You allow and make peace with the emotions that arise in reaction to those conditioned beliefs.

STEP 4

You realize the conditioned behaviors that follow these physical sensations, thoughts, and emotions are just that--programmed reactions based in nothing but habit.

As you accept each step along the way, two processes happen simultaneously.

First,
you cease to identify with the suffering self, with the experiences of mindless reaction to unexamined stimuli, and begin to recognize your authentic self as conscious, compassionate, and accepting.

Second,
you free the conditioned, reactive aspects of the personality, allowing them to return to their authentic nature.

They, too, are conscious, compassionate awareness trapped by egocentric karmic conditioning in a limited perspective. In Buddhism that perspective is referred to as

"ignorance and delusion."

Problems can never truly be resolved through acquiescence, resignation, or compromise. A resolution is reached when we each go beyond our personal limitations (which all opinions, beliefs, assumptions, and individual perspectives are) to find the place that is most compassionate to all. In other words, we will reach resolution when we move from an "I" to a "we" perspective. The agreement we are looking for is the one in which each party feels they have received more than they have given, and that they have been treated generously.

Unacceptables

What is unacceptable outside, out there, is
what is unacceptable inside.

The "unacceptables" inside are the ones
we've been taught to
beat,
    abandon,
        judge,
            and criticize ourselves for.

Whose head did it appear in?
Whose mouth did it come out of?

Seeing outside what is unacceptable inside
brings us uncomfortably close to realizing
what conditioning is set up to keep us
from ever seeing:
        that we are "that way" as well.

If we can hate others for being how they are, and if we can stay busy judging and criticizing,

perhaps we can postpone
the inevitable awareness
that what we detest in others
is what we detest in ourselves.

Have you noticed that we are so attached to life being the way we think it should be that we are consistently surprised when it isn't?

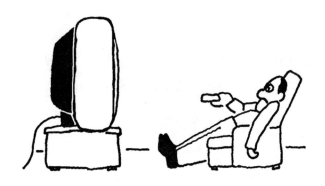

Every night we sit in front of the six o'clock news learning once again that
--someone in power is corrupt;
--priests, police officers, and public officials are not obeying the rules;
--children are being abused and exploited;
--big companies are greedy;
--people lie, cheat, and steal.

To me it is amazing that we continue to be shocked by these events and this information. How many times can we be surprised that people are the way people are rather than the way we want them to be? For that matter, how often can we be surprised that we are the way we are rather than the way we want ourselves to be?

I wonder what we would be like as a culture if we accepted that everything--ourselves, society, life--is the way it is rather than the way each of us, in our private and shared fantasies, thinks it should be.

Acceptance interferes with our ability to continue to believe that life could be the way we think it should be rather than the way it is. If life is as it is, if life does not conform to my expectations, if life will not be as I believe it must be, then what happens to me? Here I stand, holding this perspective, positioned against life unless life meets my standards, in which case I will graciously go along with it. How can I, separate from life, in opposition to it, in judgment of it, not suffer? What are the odds that life is going to be the way I say it should be all the time?

Switching Off Resistance

We cling to what's wrong, what's unacceptable, because that forms the structure of our ego identification. Who we are is defined by what we resist.

In a workshop I asked people to list the ten things they find most unacceptable in life. Then I asked them to narrow the list to seven. Uneasiness arose. When I asked them to reduce the number to five, people began to grumble that they didn't want to narrow the list any further.

"But these are things that make you miserable," I reminded them. "Your resistance to these things

1. Child abuse
2. Hunger
3. Genocide
4. Rape
5. Slavery
6. Greed
7. War
8. Torture
9. Animal abuse
10. Dishonesty

causes you great suffering. I'm asking you to let go of these sources of misery."

At three we hit downright unwillingness. Some people were ready for mutiny.

"No," they told me, "We know where this is headed. You're going to make us give them all away."

"What would be so awful about that?" I asked. "I'm suggesting you no longer have to suffer over hunger or child prostitution or sweat shops. Why wouldn't you want to give those up?"

"Because these principles are who I am. What kind of person would I be if I didn't hate injustice and cruelty?"

"So, you cling to these 'unacceptables' because they define you?"

"Yes, it's how I know I'm a good person. It's how I know I'm not like them."

Following this exchange we got to a very painful part of the discussion.

"Let me ask you this: How much of your time and energy do you give to improving these situations?"

"Not much," people mumbled. "Not enough."

"So, you hold onto these 'unacceptables' because resisting them defines who you are, yet you do little to alter them."

"Well," people protested, "It's better than doing nothing. It's better than not caring, better than seeming to say these things are okay."

Our conditioning would have us believe that not accepting an issue is the same as doing something about it, and that accepting injustice and cruelty is the same as condoning it, but it isn't. We refuse to accept that thousands of children are dying of starvation around the world everyday and think that's a contribution to the situation. But hating what's happening, trying to find someone to blame, ranting and raving about the injustice will not feed a single child.

How do we know that
child abuse,
  homelessness,
    starvation,
      genital mutilation,
       and war,
aren't a part of our world precisely to open
our hearts and move us to reach out to
people we would never know otherwise?

I'm not saying that's so, I'm just saying it's as
plausible as any other explanation.

However, whether that is or isn't so, accepting
these issues into our lives, into our world,
might open up possibilities we won't consider as
long as we're resisting.

What if the energy

we put into resisting what is

were available for addressing what is?

Without acceptance, our lives are
circumscribed by resistance.

For instance, if I'm conditioned to believe
"I'm not good enough," most of my attention
is going to be taken up gathering information
that will support my belief. In fact, the
boundaries of my life will all be marked by
"not good enough."
I'm not good enough to do that,
I'm not good enough to have that,
I'm not good enough to be that.

My entire life will happen inside the space of
"not good enough." And, to maintain my
identity, I will have to be vigilant to resist
any information that refutes my belief that
I'm not good enough.

From Unwilling to Willing

The main purpose of this book is to reveal the switch that takes us from unwilling to willing.

Let's say a part of me wants to meditate, but I don't. I know it would be good for me. I make plans and agreements, make schedules and write myself notes, call myself names, beat myself up and feel like a miserable loser. But I don't meditate. I want to, but I don't. Ever had an experience like that?

What is the mechanism holding that system in place?

RESISTANCE

What is the switch I can flip to enable me to live outside that system?

ACCEPTANCE

Resistance says:

"I don't want to be the kind of person who can't meditate if I want to meditate. I don't want to be lazy and undisciplined. I want to be the right kind of person who does the right kinds of things." So I resist being the way I am. I resist being in this situation with this problem. I dig in my heels, say no, and am stuck.

Acceptance says:

"I accept that I am the way I am. I do not need to fight my conditioning. I do not need to hate myself. I accept that I am a conditioned human, pretty much like everyone else." I say yes. Yes, this is the way I am. Yes, this is my conditioning. Yes, it is so.

When I accept ALL the ways I am--unwilling, undisciplined, lazy, guilt-ridden, resentful as well as willing, energetic, kind, compassionate, understanding--I'm no longer tying my energy up in fighting what is so, and I have a lot of energy available to me.

What shall I do with all this energy?

Well, I'd like to meditate...

Who Is Afraid, and of What?

A huge stumbling block in practicing acceptance is the fear that arises when we consider accepting ourselves. Many of us have believed since before we can remember that there are things about ourselves that are unacceptable and that to accept them would be laziness, quitting, failure. Acceptance would feel like giving up. "Can I really accept that this is the best I can do?" "Is this really how I want to spend the rest of my life?" "I only get to live once. Don't I want more? If I accept life as it is, I'll be dooming myself to a life of lack, deprivation, and misery."

However, what we notice rather quickly as we begin to practice acceptance is that we feel more relaxed and that life is more enjoyable. But what soon follows the relaxation and fun is fear. "Something must be wrong. I've stopped trying to make myself better, and I'm happier! This can't be right. What's happening to me?!"

When we step back far enough to observe the whole process, we see that there are two forces operating: egocentric karmic conditioning and authenticity, true nature. As children we were taught that to be socially acceptable we had to leave our authenticity and to identify with conditioning. As we grew we forgot that we were ever authentically ourselves and came to accept conditioning as "I/me."

Awareness practice--sitting down, getting quiet, and paying very close attention-- enables us to see that conditioned ego identity is not who we really are. When we pay close attention, conditioning is revealed (you should be this way, you have to think and feel that, good people... and so on). As we turn away from it and back to ourselves, life starts being more fun, the way life used to be, back when we were kids and not yet so thoroughly programmed.

Then comes the fear.

Why fear? Because if we practice conscious, compassionate awareness, the conditioned perspective will wither and die. Conditioning is a survival system. It does not want to die. Hence the fear. Conditioning will goad us with questions like, "Is that the best you can do? Is this how you're going to spend the rest of your life?" And just in case the answer is yes, it paints a grim picture of a dismal future. Egocentric karmic conditioning controls through fear.

If we realize conditioning tells us things to terrify us but can't deliver results, we can make it through to a relaxed, happy, enjoyable life.

Here's the clincher:
Authenticity is real,
conditioning is not real.

Essential Questions

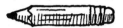

I wish everyone would ask themselves a few simple, essential questions:

What precisely is a lack of self-acceptance?

What purpose does it serve?*

How does it happen?

*If you jump to, "It helps me be a better person," ask yourself how effective it has been.

If your life isn't working
it's because
you're believing things
that aren't true
and doing things
that don't work.

As soon as you see that, you're free to
make other choices--conscious, compassionate
choices.

What stops you?

Loops

Conditioned beliefs and behaviors form loops
that we must step outside of to see. For
example:

I'm this way. I do this. I shouldn't. I try to change. I feel bad. I beat myself up. I try harder. I can't change.

The aspect of yourself you are struggling with
may be a big something or a little something,
but the result of being caught in the loop is
the same: no possibility of freedom from
dissatisfaction and suffering.

For one person the issue is food, for another it's money or relationship or family or body image or aging or emotions. The belief is that if the issue were resolved all would be well. In fact the process (the loop) would simply shift to another content (the issue). Actually, the content is so irrelevant that we could all swap and be in exactly the same place.

That's the sad joke of this whole mess!

We're all trying to figure out what the right people do, what the right character traits are, what the right life to live is, what the right thoughts to think and feelings to feel are, which religion to practice, which car to drive

and there are no right answers!

EXERCISE

Think back through your life and recall the various content that, as soon as you resolved it, would enable you to have the life you wanted. Examples: finding a mate, getting a certain job, losing weight. Make a list.

"All that is required

is that you accept

all that is unacceptable to you."

*

(from *The Key and the Name of the Key Is Willingness*)

The Function of Dissatisfaction

Dissatisfaction is pervasive in human experience. It functions as the foundation for egocentric karmic conditioning.

"Life is suffering" is a widely accepted translation of the Buddha's First Noble Truth. I suspect "dissatisfaction" may be a better word for what the Buddha was pointing at than "suffering." Perhaps the reason suffering is used rather than dissatisfaction is that suffering seems REAL and BIG, while "dissatisfaction" seems rather trivial.

But it is dissatisfaction that keeps the wheels of suffering greased and turning smoothly.

For example, dissatisfaction is at the root of our addiction to distraction. In this culture few children are taught to value being quietly present with themselves. As adults, we are so uncomfortable with quiet, unscheduled time that we will do almost anything to escape it. We say we value "free time," but mostly we

value it only after we are exhausted by doing
so much (and feel we have earned a rest.
But that's another story). So most of us,
unless we have no spark of energy left in
our bodies, are addicted to having something
going on around us all the time to distract us
from being quietly with ourselves. Marketing
and advertising experts know this. Music plays
in elevators, on hold on the telephone, in
gyms, offices, lobbies, restaurants. Televisions
blare in airports, stores, and hospitals.
Magazines and newspapers and cell phones are
available to occupy us when we have a few
moments with "nothing to do." We are
inundated with advertisements for more
products and services than we could ever
use. We must have the latest labor-saving
devices, the newest
technology, this season's
fashions...

all to feed our chronic dissatisfaction.

Conditioned habits, thoughts, and behaviors suck our energy. But we can learn not to give our attention and awareness to distraction, and our reward is to have all the energy we want. When we don't fritter our energy away, we can have as much energy for life, bliss, joy, enthusiasm, inspiration, compassion, wisdom, love, giving, and sharing as we can contain. We can even "expand the container" so we're able to receive more.

Or we can allow egocentric karmic conditioning to siphon it off in distraction, reinforcing dissatisfaction. The choice is ours when we're conscious.

For most of us more of life works than doesn't work. People we love get sick and die, we lose a job or become ill, but most of the time we're not having those experiences. Most of us have enough to eat, a place to live, and medical care when we need it. Our suffering is not so much from the circumstances of our lives as from being dissatisfied with our lives.

I call these the "yabbuts."

--- Yes, I have a job, but I hate it.
--- Yes, I make a decent living, but everything is so expensive, I still can't afford the things I want.
--- Yes, I'm here doing what I wanted to come here to do, but I'm not enjoying it the way I thought I would.
--- Yes, I have a wonderful, challenging job, but I'm too tired at the end of the day to do the things I want to do.
--- Yes, I loved this outfit when I bought it, but now I'm not sure it's right for me.
--- Yes, I have medical care, but it's so expensive and it doesn't cover everything.
--- Yes, I have friends, but they bore me/ don't pay enough attention to me/ live too far away/ aren't there when I need them/ are too demanding.
--- Add your own

Dissatisfaction is the glue that holds
egocentric karmic conditioning together.
When I'm dissatisfied, I'm <u>ME.</u>
"I don't like that, I don't want that, there's
something wrong with them, there's
something wrong with me, this is not
acceptable, I can't stand that, I wish I had
more_____, I wish I had less_____, the
world shouldn't be like it is..."

Dissatisfaction
is the cause of suffering
we can most easily eliminate by accepting.

When we accept, life can be the way it is and
we can enjoy it. The bad news, from the
perspective of egocentric karmic conditioning,
is that when we're accepting we are not the
center of the universe. Acceptance tends to
do away with the building blocks of egocentric
karmic conditioning, which are urgency, fear,
lack and deprivation, and the "something
wrong" that needs to be fixed.

Snug Little Ego Comfort Zone

We often react as if life is attacking us. "I'm not going to be able to stand this," we fret as life pushes us beyond our snug little ego comfort zone.

But we have no evidence of not being able to handle anything life brings us.

How do we know that? We've handled everything so far.

"Yabbut, what if..." the voices shout.

Ah, that's a projection into an imaginary future.

Is there anything I can't handle right now, in this moment?

No.

Okay, there's the answer.

Waking Up into Awareness

First thing in the morning is a great time to observe the interplay between conditioning and awareness. Awareness never sleeps, but most people wake up into conditioning. Although the body and mind are not quite awake, conditioning is already at work.

It is possible to wake up "identified" with awareness, before the habitual reactions of body and mind start up, and watch conditioning do what it does. (This can be practiced all the time once you get the hang of it.) All that is required is that you realize you are not conditioning. As soon as you disidentify from conditioning and identify with awareness, all wisdom and clarity is available.

If you do not lose focus,
if you remain conscious,
you can watch conditioning
do what it does
until you have observed
and seen through
all that has caused you
to defend against life
and resist who you are.

How Conditioning Works:
Threatening the Dictator

Conditioning is difficult to deal with because it is so deeply embedded. It's as if little grooves are made in our brains that cause us to see what we see, hear what we hear, believe what we believe, react as we react, assume what we assume, experience what we experience. Every movement, thought, feeling, conclusion, decision, perception, belief (along with everything else we could put in the endless list of how a human being reacts to its environment) is programmed, ingrained, learned, trained. The difficulty we face is that it is a part of our conditioning not to recognize our conditioning.*

*For more on this subject see *The Mind and the Brain: Neuroplasticity and the Power of Mental Force* by Jeffrey M. Schwartz and Sharon Begley; ReganBooks, 2002.

Egocentric karmic conditioning is a survival system that was created in childhood in response to a need.

When a need arises, children do anything necessary to get that need met. No sacrifice is too big, no abandonment too painful, no treasure too dear to surrender.

Sometimes this works to get the need met; sometimes it doesn't. And now, as adults, those childhood responses are still controlling our lives in harmful, painful, suffering ways that NEVER work. It's like the revolutionary leader who frees his people from slavery and then becomes a ruthless dictator. We blindly believe he is supporting us even though he is now enslaving us.

In adult lives, childhood egocentric karmic conditioning creates a world of win/lose, right/wrong, good/bad, succeed/fail, the thrill of victory and the agony of defeat.

Here's an example of the way it works: Conditioning identifies something as important to succeed at, and then makes sure we fail most of the time. Why? Remember, it is a SURVIVAL system and it must constantly create situations that it can survive. That's just what it does. It's not helpful, not intelligent, not a good life plan, but it's deeply ingrained in each of us and cannot be short-circuited or transcended without clear awareness of how it operates. Awareness practice reveals conditioning's strategy for what it is.

Let's use public speaking as our example. There you are, a good person trying hard, and part of what you do is public speaking. From conditioning's perspective, your worth as a human being rides on how well you perform. That kind of pressure guarantees that a good

part of the time you will not meet the standards imposed by conditioning. Because this is a system designed to keep you the person who survived a long past childhood, you can know that no matter how proficient you are at public speaking, the conditioned survival system will rate your performance as inferior or worse most of the time. Occasionally, it will throw you a crumb, just often enough to keep you in its clutches.

You are never
going to win this game!

When you see this,
when you accept that the
system is set up that way,

you're free to stop trying
to win a rigged contest.

Conditioning fighting to keep
control of your life
is an ugly battle.

(Consider those images of God and the devil
wrestling for your soul, Saint John of the
Cross's "dark night of the soul": this is
serious work we are doing here.) Yes, when
you're identified with conditioning, you don't
want to wake up and end suffering. Yes, when
you're identified with conditioning, it wins. And,
NO! The battle does not go on forever. It will
get very intense. The voices of conditioning
will try to convince you it will last forever
and you won't be able to stay the course,
but the voices lie. One day you'll pop up
through the morass of suffering and struggle
and know that, even if it catches you again
for a short time, you've seen the lie and
you're free of it.

It is perfectly acceptable, even encouraged,
to actively pursue conditioning in order to get
a closer look at it. For instance, emotional
reactions that have been with us for years

are baggage.
Old baggage.
Torn and
tattered

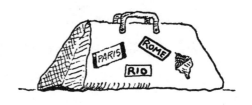

baggage. For the purpose of seeing through how you were conditioned, you don't have to wait for life to provide the circumstances to have those old responses. If anger is an issue for you, go where you know people will say or do things that will set you off. To watch yourself being shy, seek out groups of strangers.

Being in the present is going to give us all the information we need about what to do or not to do. We can drop old patterns, let them go, and be here, where we are now. Conditioning doesn't want us to leave the past behind and sends big danger signals. But be assured, threatening the dictator is not dangerous. Scary, perhaps, but not dangerous.
Could save your life.
Could give you freedom.

Why Wake Up?

Once we've been socialized, conditioning is the "default setting" in life. When we're not paying attention, we automatically revert to our learned orientation. Then we "wake up" and find ourselves conscious, present, aware, and we experience life as it is. The next moment we fail to practice being awake, conditioning grabs the wheel. Over and over again. This is a real argument for a consistent awareness practice. Not because we <u>should</u> practice, but because we know that's the quickest route to waking up, and life is way more fun when we're here for it.

Let's take an example of conditioned behavior and dissect it to see what we can learn.

You decide to bake a cake. You get excited about it. You read the recipe and make a list of ingredients, and you go to the store and buy them.

Chocolate Cake

2 cups sugar
1 3/4 cups flour
3/4 cup unsweetened cocoa
1 1/2 tsp. baking soda
1 1/2 tsp. baking powder
1 tsp. salt
1 cup boiling water

2 eggs or egg substitute
1/2 cup soft tofu,
  blended in food processor
1/2 cup soymilk
1/2 cup applesauce
2 tsp. vanilla

Pre-heat oven to 350°. Oil and flour two 9" cake pans or a 9x13" rectangular pan. Sift dry ingredients, then combine them in a large bowl. Add eggs, tofu, soymilk, applesauce, and vanilla. Beat on medium speed for 2 minutes. Remove from mixer and stir in boiling water. Pour into prepared pans and bake 30-35 minutes for round pans; 35-40 minutes for rectangular pan.

You have everything you need, including the right cake pans and an oven that works. You spread everything out on the counter, tie on your apron, wash your hands, and you're ready to go. Then you hear a voice say...

Do you think those voices are on your side?
Do you think they want you to succeed?

NO!
AND NOTHING WILL EVER BE DIFFERENT
UNTIL YOU STOP
GIVING THOSE VOICES
CONTROL OF YOUR LIFE.

They are the conditioned voices of ego
identity survival maintenance. I call them the
voices of self-hatred. They want you to fail
and suffer because that's the way to keep
you small and afraid and "safe." They have no
good, helpful, instructive, supportive
information for you.

It's true for all of us. Whether the voices
are shouting or whispering, whether the
information comes as voices in your head or
sensations in your body, anything aimed at
keeping you fearful, closed, isolated, anxious,
insecure, and upset is self-hatred and has

NOTHING GOOD TO ADD TO YOUR LIFE !

Self-Talk

Self-talk can be the things you say and hear inside your head, and self-talk can be revealed in what we unconsciously say to others. Every unconscious thought is part of a brainwashing system. Our conditioning is maintained by a constant stream of unconscious, self-reinforcing information. For instance, how many times each day must I be compared to others who are more successful, more attractive, smarter, or happier to get it that I am lesser? Self-talk need not be verbalized. I look at two attractive, well-dressed people walking down the street, talking, laughing, smiling, and the instant comparison proves that I am an unattractive loser. Self-talk can come in the form of a feeling. Nothing is said, but the way I feel means that I'll never get it right and everyone hates me.

If I have a voice saying, "You are a fat, disgusting pig,"

and I believe that voice and feel bad because I believe it's true, I'm miserable. However, when I realize it's just a voice, that it has no substance, that it's like a parrot repeating

SQUAWK
SQUAWK
SQUAWK

without thought or knowledge, that it's a habit, that what it says is not true, I have a whole different relationship with it. Now I can look at the part of me that listens to that message and feels the pain, and I can begin to mentor that part of myself. As I bring conscious compassionate awareness to this whole unexamined ball of suffering, I begin to gain some perspective. Everybody has these voices!

I don't need to take this personally. I am not being singled out because I'm the only bona fide loser on the planet! This is just something that goes on, like trash or traffic or tricky telephone systems designed to keep me from ever talking to another person. Whew. I can free up some energy to use somewhere else.

If you think about it, it's what the voices are telling you that makes you miserable, not how you are. If the voices would stop talking, if you weren't being beaten up with how it should be, if all this didn't mean anything, would you be suffering as you are?

Life is glorious.
Almost no one experiences life.

We experience conditioned mind
and think that's life.

The King and the Servant

Here's a wonderful little tale that offers a clear picture of the relationship between our authentic nature and egocentric karmic conditioning.

Once upon a time there was a great king who lived in a castle. He had a servant whom he appointed to tend the door of the castle.

For a while everything was good in the king's palace, but soon the doorman began bringing troubling news, frightening stories of people who wanted to kill the king and take away his riches.

The king, upon first hearing these tales, told the doorman, "Stand aside. I'll go out and confront these enemies immediately."

But the doorman refused to move. "You can't go out there sir," he said. "If you do your enemies will kill you."

"What shall I do?" asked the king.

"You must stay inside and let me deal

with them," said the doorman.

And so the king allowed the doorman to go out and speak to these enemies.

Each time the doorman came back to the king he had more horrible tales to tell, frightening the king more and more.

At first the king simply stayed inside his castle. But as time went on, he felt safer secluding himself in one wing, far from the main activities. Eventually, he confined himself to a small closet in the servants' quarters.

For many years the king lived in the closet and listened through the door to the doorman's reports of all the dangers outside. The small, cramped, dark closet became his whole world. To protect the king, the doorman had a slot cut in the bottom of the door to slide food through, so the door would never have to be opened.

One day after the king had spent a third of his life in the closet, he heard a knock on the door. One of the maids who tended to the castle spoke to him.

"Sir," she said, "I can't keep silent anymore. The doorman is living like a king, and you are living like his prisoner."

"He's protecting me," said the king.

"It's not true," said the maid. "There were never any enemies you couldn't have dealt with. He's been lying to you sir, in order to take over your castle for himself."

"No enemies?" said the king, unbelieving.

"There were those who would have tried to harm you, but none were as smart or as dangerous as the very one who promised to protect you. You must come out and put him in his place."

"But I can't," said the king. "If I do, I'll be killed."

"Sir," said the maid, "The greatest danger you face is dying here in this closet. Even if you were killed by your enemies, wouldn't that be preferable to dying here without ever having lived?"

The king was silent.

Finally the maid said, "You must decide. I've told you the truth, now you must act on it."

The king heard her turn the key and unlock his door.

When he finally gathered the courage to peek out into the corridor all was quiet. He stepped out and made his way to the castle proper. What he found there shocked him. The doorman was sitting on his throne, and all the servants were bringing him food and drink and tending to his every need.

When the doorman saw the king he jumped up and began reciting his litany of fears and threats. He took hold of the king's elbow and tried to guide him back to the closet.

But the king refused. He shook off the doorman's hand and bellowed: "I am the king of the realm. You are all my subjects."

He looked directly at the doorman. "You, servant, have deceived me and for this crime I banish you from my kingdom forevermore." He then ordered the guards to throw the man out.

From that day forward, the king moved freely through all the rooms of his palace. They belonged to him and he was comfortable in them all. He would marvel the rest of his days at the deception that had ensnared him and at the fact that if it had not been for the maid who whispered the truth to him, he would have lost his life one slow moment at a time.

Because of what she had done, the king summoned the maid, married her, and made her queen over his realm. Together they ruled and lived happily ever after.*

* Troy Chapman. Reprinted from *Inspirit, The Newsletter of The Lifeful Way.* PO Box 731, Narberth, PA 19072. Inspirit01@earthlink.net. www.lifefulway.org

PART TWO

How to Accept

Terrifying Tumble, Graceful Dive

  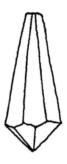

There's a story about a spiritual teacher who had a fine collection of prisms that hung across an expanse of windows in his living room. A student cleaning the windows knocked down the whole lot, and they smashed to bits on the floor. The student was terrified and distraught. The teacher came in, saw what had happened, paused for a moment and then laughed. The student was astonished. "It's all right," the teacher said. "I had those for pleasure, not for suffering."

The teacher in this story illustrates that it is possible to find ourselves in the middle of a fall, and instead of tightening up with resistance, to let go, to accept what is happening, and to turn a terrifying tumble into a graceful dive.

Acceptance is not difficult.
It is not complex or confusing.

Acceptance is as simple and as easy as letting go of a long deep breath and relaxing all the muscles in the body. It's resistance that's hard. Fighting life, going against the grain, is arduous. Tensing up and saying "no" to life is painful.

I describe acceptance as happening with the head up and resignation as happening with the head down. With head down, miserable, defeated, cynical, bitter, we can tell instantly that we are caught in resistance. Head up is associated with energy, enthusiasm, freedom, and possibility.

Letting Go into Acceptance

What if you accepted everything about
yourself? "What would I do then?" people ask.
To me a more interesting question is, "Who
would you be?" Or perhaps, "How would the
world look?"

What will happen if you let go of resistance?
Will all your worst fears come to pass?
Will you become lazy and self-indulgent and
egocentric?
Will your world go to hell in
a handbasket?
Will good be vanquished and
evil prevail?

How about finding out?

STUDENT

The more I look, the more I see I don't really accept anything. I pretend to accept, but dig a little deeper and part of me always wishes things were different--that I was better-looking, richer, more powerful, etc. My problem is that I believe what my ego tells me. Come to think of it, I guess my ego is incapable of accepting anything. Maybe I am looking for acceptance in the wrong place--in my head instead of in my heart.

GUIDE

What is it that wishes for things to be different? What wants more beauty, riches, and power? Would that be the ego or the heart? As we become familiar with the movement back and forth between those two, we can sense when we're in one or the other. Acceptance, well-being, expansiveness equals heart. Nonacceptance, fear, hatred, closed down equals egocentric karmic conditioning.

How does my body feel? What am I experiencing emotionally? What's going on with my mind? A quick check-in can tell me who is at the wheel. And, here's the wonderful, magical nature of how all this works: that check-in itself is the movement that places me squarely in my heart. That's why we meditate. Once we know the expansive acceptance of here/now, all we need is to check in and, poof! we're home free.

✷✷

Acceptance Is a Doorway

When we accept--

⇒ acknowledging the existence of something in our life whether we like and approve of it or not,

⇒ acknowledging that it exists because we are creating it and holding its existence in place,

⇒ acknowledging that we are projecting it--

then we are in a position to respond to it rather than reacting to it from our preconceived beliefs and assumptions about how life should be.

Everything we accept
is available to us
to see,
to use,
to learn from,
to let go.

Acceptance is a doorway,
a portal to what lies beyond,
to all that exists on the other side
of a wall of resistance.

That can be something huge, such as a
locked-away memory from a childhood trauma,
or something as simple as flexibility for a
body locked in fear of injury.
For example, if I have a certain trait--
   I don't stand up for myself
   I want to have everything under control
   I have no talent for organization
   I can't say no if someone needs me
and I do not accept this about myself, I
struggle. I read books, take classes, and go to
therapy. I judge and punish myself. I try to
change and fail.

If I embrace in compassion the parts of me
who have such difficulty with this trait, I can
say to myself, "Yes, I have a hard time with
this, but having this trait does not make me

a bad person, it makes me a person who is struggling and suffering." At this point transformation is possible. When resistance, judgment, and punishment are no longer part of the picture, the struggle ends.

Acceptance is the same as the heart being open. How could life be made better by closing our hearts?

Seeing through Illusion

We struggle with acceptance not because circumstances are difficult, but because we've been conditioned to resist. Resistance is essential to ego, to our sense of being a separate self. In refusing to accept what is, "I" am in a critical position relative to life. I am more important than it. I have the power. I am in control. Of course this is nothing but illusion, but that's the way it feels.

Why do I keep telling my teenage children to clean their rooms when I know it will never happen? If you want to know the answer to any "why?"  question, look to see what you get in your life as a result of what you're doing or not doing, accepting or not accepting. What do I get? I get to be right, I get to be self-righteous, I get to feel like a bad parent, I get to be a victim, I don't have to focus on far more

upsetting life issues, I get to let off a lot of
steam, I get...

Why don't I meditate when I know it will
make my life easier?
I get to feel wrong, I get to feel like a
victim (why do I have to do this?), I get to
blame myself when my life doesn't work, I
get to be in control (I know why my life is
hard), I get to be right (I never have been
able to stick with anything), I get to...

Why can't I be better with money?
I get to feel out of control, I get to feel like
a victim, I don't have to take responsibility, I
get to feel "less than," I have an excuse, I
can stay in my old familiar place in life, I...

When I refuse to accept--that my kids don't
like housework, that maintaining a meditation
practice is hard for me, that I'm not a skilled
money manager--I cringe and try to avoid:
"I'm afraid. I can't do this. I'm not capable. I
don't have what it takes."

Or I deny and puff with righteous indignation:
"I hate this. Life's just not fair. I try but I
get no support."

If I am willing to find out how "I cannot
accept" works, I pursue, I watch, I notice, I
explore, I challenge.

When I hear voices in my head that say,
"I cannot work this computer.
Technology is beyond me.
I'm not scientifically inclined.
It's too hard, I don't get it,
I don't want to, I'm afraid,"

I stop to consider, how can this be so? Small
children can work computers. What is really
stopping me? What is this resistance actually
about? I want to know exactly what "too
hard" means and where it lives.

A Clearer Perspective

The first step we can take toward living in acceptance instead of resistance is to accept that we resist. Yep, I resist. It's a fact.

We begin by learning to see clearly where we are and to face and accept everything that arises when we turn full attention to our conditioned self. This kind of nonjudgmental observing is available, but it is not the lens through which we usually look. How do we find a different, clearer perspective? How do we get outside ego? The most effective way I know is meditation.

 Meditation is the easiest way to practice seeing what is. We sit down, sit still, and notice everything while allowing everything to be exactly as it is. If we are patient, if we are willing to "wait and see," that is exactly what will happen--we will see it all.

Ego, conditioning, does not like to be scrutinized and will fight back. If we practice breathing and noticing and letting go and accepting, we will learn to watch all that arises as it arises and to continue to watch it as it passes away. There are those who view this as passive, but only those who have never tried it.

Seeing clearly and accepting all we see does not mean we will choose to have everything about us go on as before. (Even if we wanted that, it would be impossible. The seeing itself will have changed us.) Often there are things about ourselves that we accept, have sympathy for, understand completely, and still want to work toward making different. Let's say that I am afraid I will be laughed at or rejected if I ask for what I want, and that I have fully, compassionately accepted this about myself. Does this mean I spend the rest of my life not asking for what I want? No, indeed not.

With acceptance
comes the ability to effect changes
simply because I want to,
not because there is
something wrong
with me that should be fixed.

Our attitude of mind toward ourselves might
be summed up in this way:

"I love you exactly as you are,
and I will help you be however
you want to be."

EXERCISE

Write down a behavior you have that causes you difficulty, discomfort, or concern, probably something people have commented on throughout your life, very likely an object of self-improvement for you. Common examples might be eating, exercising, working, or talking too much or too little; addictive or compulsive behaviors such as alcohol consumption and smoking; patterns of relating to others. I will ask you to work with this behavior as you read through this section.

Describe the behavior as briefly as possible. Examples:

"I always have to be doing something. When people are eating I'm the one up serving. After the meal I'm the one cleaning up. People ask me to sit down and rest, but I can't."

"I've tried to quit smoking since high school. I know it's bad for me, but I can't quit. If I'm not smoking I eat. I have to have something in my mouth and in my hands."

Okay? Short and clear.

The Sequence to Watch

The progression we will explore in practicing acceptance through conscious, compassionate awareness goes back 2500 years to the Buddha. You can discover for yourself, in yourself, this sequence:

1) Movement. Everything is moving all the time. It may appear that some things (such as rocks) are not moving, but it's our limited perception that makes an object seem immobile.

2) Sensation. As sentient beings we experience that constant movement of life in our bodies. Air and fluids shift and flow, muscles contract and release, joints rotate as we go about doing the things we do. Sounds vibrate in our ears; our eyes dilate, tear, and blink. Even more sensitive aspects of our physical forms respond constantly to energy fluctuations and vibrations we are unaware of.

3) Thought. We have a thought about a sensation: "It's too loud." "It's too quiet." "I'm cold." "They're wrong."

4) Emotion. We have a feeling in response to the thought: "I don't like this."

5) Behavior. We have a karmically conditioned behavior in reaction to the feeling: "I've got to get out of here."

Identifying this progression within ourselves will enable us to accept anything. The reason is simple. All struggle is a struggle to accept ourselves. Our lack of acceptance appears to be about other people, places, and things, but it is not. Resistance to accepting the most intellectual, commonplace, esoteric, or concrete thing comes down to "me," that little ego identity attempting to survive as a self separate from life.

It would be marvelously helpful if we experienced these five steps as discrete events. Awareness practice would be very simple if each step lasted five minutes or so, but they arise and disappear more like socks in a washer or vermicelli boiling in water, moving fast in a confusing tangle. It is not necessary to know what is going on with all of them, just with one. If the first awareness is in the body, once we get comfortable with the physical sensations, our attention is freed up to bring awareness to the mind and the emotions. Soon we are able to recognize the whole ball of conditioned reactions arising at once, we know what it is, and we don't need to resist it. As we continue to pay attention, we realize that we are not that ball of conditioned reactions, but rather we are the conscious, compassionate awareness noticing it. All aspects arise at once, and any of them can be a doorway to freedom.

The Buddha taught us to end suffering through contemplation of body, feelings, mind, and mind objects. As we identify more with conscious compassionate awareness and less with conditioning, we are increasingly able to enjoy gathering information and making discoveries. As we discover that conditioning is not who we are, we take it less personally, and we enjoy seeing it for what it is. As we see it for what it is, it loses power over us.

A Pair of Pitfalls

FEAR

As soon as we start to watch, fear will arise.
Why? Because we are conditioned to be
afraid. But keep watching, and the experience
we call fear will dissipate. However, if you get
caught up in a story about *what* you're afraid
of, you will be in the grip of conditioning.
Instead, pay really close attention. Evoke that
spiritual warrior! Sit and watch until the story
subsides, along with the sensations it evokes,
the thoughts, the emotions, and you are
sitting in sheer joy. "Hot darn! This works."

KNOWING

Please be aware that watching is not the
same as "knowing ahead of time."

In mystery stories, and in science, we enjoy
the process of discovering, through gathering
evidence, that something is altogether
different from what it seemed. We are less
fond of such discoveries as they apply to
ourselves.

Suffering is held in place by illusion and assumption. We assume that what we're thinking, seeing, and feeling is real, in the that's-just-how-it-is sense of real. But it appears real only until we examine it closely.

Embrace the Unacceptable

We're familiar with the expression "What you resist, persists."

We are less familiar with the old Zen expression, "What you try to cling to skedaddles."

But we can see how this works when we examine how structures are maintained through resistance. For instance,

I am a cranky person.
I don't want to be a cranky person.
All my energy goes into
trying not to be cranky.
(Of course, this makes me very cranky.)

What is impossible to know is whether I am cranky because I simply am, or if I am cranky because all my attention is on how I'm cranky and don't want to be.

The way out of this impasse?
Turn around and move
toward
the unacceptable behavior.
Embrace it.
Pursue it.

"Okay crankiness, talk to me.
What's going on?
How can I help?
What do you need?"

Soon I have difficulty maintaining the dreaded
behavior. Why? Because when I turn around,
drop the resistance and bring consciousness to
the matter, the whole dynamic changes. I'm no
longer holding the sensations of crankiness in
place through resistance. Now I'm looking for
crankiness, inviting it in so that I can embrace
it...

but I can't find it!

So...

on to the next behavior: "I eat all the time."

Do I? I'll watch and see.

And I repeat the same process of acceptance with this issue.

Finding the Switch

Whatever the suffering is, it's triggered by something. What is that trigger? Can you find what is fueling the desire for the behavior? What is the switch (sensation) marked food or rage or procrastinate, etc.? When the switch is off, no behavior, no reaction to eat or yell or avoid. When the switch is on, behavior, now! If you can't find the switch, if the switch gets turned on and you don't know how to turn it off, you're sunk. All the good intentions, self-improvement, and merciless beatings will not help you one iota.

I'm going to give you one of those big hints we're always hoping to get in life, a secret of the universe in the form of a parable.

A student came to a master seeking freedom from suffering. The master gave the student a fish and sent her into her room to observe it. A few moments later the student, excited about the prospect of enlightenment, dashed out to report the length, breadth, and color of the fish. The master explained that that wasn't what he meant by paying attention. The kind of observation he had in mind is much more than a quick perusal; it's being deeply aware of and present with the object. Back the student went. An hour later she returned with more information. Again the teacher rejected her superficial examination. The next day the scenario was repeated, and the next, and the next. Finally, the teacher realized the student had not appeared for quite some time and sent a monk to fetch her. When the monk knocked on the door, the student called out, "Please go away. I'm very busy observing."

Okay, grab your fish! Now we're going to look more closely at movement, sensation, thought, emotion, and behavior.

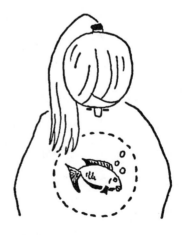

1· MOVEMENT

 Movement, the first step, is literally the constant motion of the universe. Galaxies whirl, planets spin, oceans surge, blood courses through bodies, thoughts race through minds, subatomic particles blink into and out of existence--all aspects of movement.

"...The scientist has discovered that everything is in constant flux by examining the external world, [while] the meditator will discover this same truth inside his or her own body..."

-Wes Nisker

Within this context, the human body can be thought of as a receiving station, a sensitive device that registers the movement of energy, interprets it, and takes action. This faculty, it seems to me, is the genesis of the illusion of separation, the illusion that there is an "I" separate from everything else, a someone who stands apart from existence. (This is also, it seems to me, the genesis of suffering.)

Scientists and mystics know that there is no observer separate from the observed:

"The belief in an external world independent of the perceiving subject is the basis of all natural science. Since, however, sense perception only gives information of this external world or of 'physical reality' indirectly, we can only grasp the latter by speculative means. It follows from this that our notions of physical reality can never be final. We must always be ready to change these notions--that is to say, the axiomatic basis of physics--in order to do justice to perceived facts in the most perfect way logically."

-Albert Einstein

"Relativity and quantum theory have shown that it has no meaning to divide the observing apparatus from what is observed."

-David Bohm

"We generally distinguish between inner and outer, but...the distinction is no more than a form of thought construction.... Change the position, and what is inner is outer, and what is outer is inner."

-D. T. Suzuki

"While the Tathagata, in his teaching, constantly makes use of conceptions and ideas about them, disciples should keep in mind the unreality of all such conceptions and ideas. They should recall that the Tathagata, in making use of them in explaining the Dharma always uses them in the semblance of a raft that is of use only to cross a river. As the raft is of no further use after the river is crossed, it should be discarded. So these arbitrary conceptions of things and about things should be wholly given up as one attains enlightenment."

-The Buddha

* All quotes are from *Einstein and Buddha: The Parallel Sayings*, edited by Thomas J. McFarlane; Seastone, 2002

When we know, even intellectually, that our sense of separateness is an illusion, we discover that we can step back from the illusion into a less "identified" perspective. From here, with practice, we gain the ability to observe sensation, thought, emotion, and behavior--the next four steps in the process.

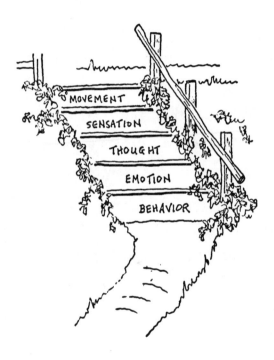

2·SENSATION

In observing sensations, we're attempting to see what's there *before* the mind labels an experience and reaches conclusions about it.

We are attempting to be present
as sensation arises.
This is a fresh perspective,
a "new" mind.

Paradoxically, this new mind requires us to get out of our heads; it is exceedingly difficult to get past our conditioned ideas to the sensations behind them. In the process I'm describing, we're looking for the sensation *before* the thought "I'm hungry," or the emotion "I feel anxious," and the behavior that follows. Actually, we're looking for the sensation prior to any sense of "I."

When looking at the issue you chose on page 96, it can be helpful to write down everything that precedes the behavior we're concerned about. If my issue is smoking, before I light a cigarette, before I pick up the pack, I write down everything I notice about how I feel in my body. Where is there tightness or tension? What's my breathing like? My heartbeat?  Write down anything and everything, whether it seems pertinent or not. Each time I feel the urge to have a cigarette, I add to my list. This develops my ability to pay closer attention. As the many sensations become more familiar, the initial sensation becomes more accessible.

It is important to have no conclusions about any of this. Conclusions happen in the mind, not in the body. We are research scientists. Being convinced of the results before we do the experiments is not good science. We're going back, back, back to that first impulse that sets the whole chain of events in motion. To do this, our attention must be very subtle.

It may be helpful to consider that our suffering is not in the sensation itself but in our conclusions, our beliefs, the meaning we assign to the sensation. The suffering is not in the body. Each time you think you know something, consider that what thinks it knows is conditioning. What we're looking for happens before knowing or understanding, before labels or ideas--just a tiny sensation, but one that initiates an avalanche of reaction. It is in your interest not to leave this tiny instigator in the hands of a merely intellectual understanding.

Take your time to find out about the sensation. Urgency may rise up to try to convince you to quit.
"This is taking too long."
"How important can it be, anyway?"
"There are more important things to do."

Perhaps more efficiently than anything else, urgency keeps us in ignorance and delusion. You're looking, seeing, noticing, digging deeper, and a voice says, "You're wasting your time," and awareness is abandoned. Don't fall for it. This process of observation leads directly to clarity, and you can't get there sooner by hurrying.

If we don't get clear on a sensation level, we'll be like a person trying to cook a meal who gets caught up in playing with the ingredients and reading the packages rather than following the recipe and making the meal. If we don't get back to the beginning, we waste our time and energy shifting the content around.

Here's the bottom line for all of us and the reason we must, if we're to do this work, meditate: We must

practice sitting still through the sensations
until we realize that
1) they don't mean what we've thought they
meant, and
2) we don't need to do anything in reaction,
because they have no power.

We sit, we breathe, we watch the sensations
come into existence, we watch our conditioned
reactions (thought, emotion, behavior), we
breathe, we watch the sensations pass away.
Freedom.

It's helpful to remember that the body has
no issues. All of our issues exist in the
conditioned mind. But through paying attention
to the body we can become conscious of the
physical experiences that link directly into
conditioned patterns of behavior.

The experience that will free us is the
moment when we get it that the sensation
that lies at the bottom of a conditioned
reaction to life does not mean what we
assume it means.

The reason we can't get to that realization
is that we are

        so caught up in,

           so attached to,

              so identified with

       THE STORY.

"I'm the way I am because my parents
were/said/thought/believed and did _____
to me, and now I'm this way and I can't help
myself."
         NO!

The reason "I am the way I am" is that I
was conditioned to avoid a feeling I had as a
child, and now as an adult I am still avoiding a
feeling I have never stopped to examine.

We suffer trying to avoid a feeling that is
only a feeling and means nothing. We are
controlled by fear of our feelings.

If we drop the story for only a moment we
can realize the sensations in our bodies

aren't dangerous. The difficulty is that the story constitutes the identity of a "self," which, to survive childhood, was required to become "separate." Both self and separation are illusions, created to meet the needs of the child. The fact that they are illusory does not make it easy to let them go--far from it. Even though the needs that brought the "separate self" into being no longer exist, even though that sense of separation is the cause of suffering, our dependence on each of those stories is
lifelong,
desperate,
and unconscious.

Until now.

Please note that I'm not encouraging you to believe that the stories aren't true any more than I would encourage you to defend them. Allow each story to be there. Accept it. Allow the person invested in the story to continue believing it. Accept that part of you.

Allow the voices to argue and defend. Accept them. Know that great emotion may accompany your exploration of the triggers for your conditioning. Accept the emotions.

As you're allowing and accepting, keep one eye on what happens in your body. Feel the energy move around, notice where the energy gets blocked, stuck. Feel the places of pain, tightness, and tension. Where do you contract? The story is going right on, very possibly at a higher volume. As a good detective, you nod and listen. But you're not listening to the content of the story. You're not believing the story and getting caught up in all the beliefs and assumptions and meanings. You're observing the whole gestalt and asking yourself, "What is behind this? What is keeping this structure in place? What triggers it each time it comes into existence?"

Stay with the sensation until you find the exact location that triggers the whole story. "This sensation means I must feel such and

such, think such and such, and act so and so."
That's the start button. One second you're
not having the experience, the next one you
are. What connects the dots?

EXERCISE

Consider the issue you are working with.
Where in your body do you feel the
sensations associated with this behavior?

STUDENT

Where do I feel the sensation? When I'm
eating, I feel a ravenous emptiness in my
throat. I feel like I want my mouth and my
throat to be as full as they can be. The
image is a hungry baby bird with a large, open
mouth. I feel desperate to stuff as much in
as possible, to feed the emptiness. It feels
as though no matter how much I can scoop
into my mouth, the emptiness will never be
filled. (That's probably the truest realization
I've had around this topic.) Once I've eaten,
my stomach aches with the discomfort. The
fullness that I have longed for in my throat
is now in my stomach and feels horrible.

GUIDE

"Ravenous emptiness" is a thought, not a
feeling. What I want you to close in on is the
fact that those sensations don't mean what
you've thought they mean. You know that is
so because they never actually result in what
you think they will to result in. Those familiar
sensations result in horrible discomfort. If
you could associate "horrible discomfort" with

those sensations you get when you're eating, you'd stop eating! The conditioned connection is eating = relief = pleasure = well-being. The assumption is, "I feel bad with this empty space, but as soon as it's filled, I'll feel good." As you know that's not true.

As soon as you get it from your own experience that those sensations in your throat do not mean "shovel food in as quickly as possible," your life is going to be very, very different. If you were conditioned to believe those sensations mean "Sing," or "Say I love you to myself," or "Have a massage," your life would be transformed. I'm not encouraging you to program yourself with a different message. I just want you to see that the connection between those feelings and that behavior is

bogus.

Stay with it. The resistance will be mighty, because what you're attempting to see, is the exact mechanism that allows conditioning to keep you in suffering.

**

It is difficult to come up with words to describe the sensations without sliding into a story. When we really feel the sensations, words can seem quite useless. As soon as I choose a word, I know that's not quite it. I'm left with, "Well, it's sort of like___," or "You know, it's similar to___." But it isn't.

Our lives are being controlled

by sensations in our bodies

that we cannot explain,

cannot accurately label,

and don't understand.

How have we missed this?

⇨

We've been taught to focus on the story. We move the pieces of the puzzle around, we look at them from different angles, and we believe that will lead to clarity. It won't, because the piece we need to solve the puzzle has been missing. The missing piece is the sensation that triggers the cycle of conditioned response. Again, rather than trying to avoid or change anything, we're now focusing attention in a place we've never looked before.

STUDENT

My compulsive behavior is looking at women's bodies to judge their sexual attractiveness. I notice many different sensations with this activity, but they are not unique sensations-- drowsiness if it's after lunch, greater clarity in the morning. I cannot attribute any sensations to the activity itself. In fact, while looking at a woman, I lose contact with sensations. I am "in my head" and must make an effort to notice sensations again.

GUIDE

You will need to pay closer attention. The sensations are there. You're being bamboozled by conditioning. Big hint: This activity exists precisely so you will "lose contact with sensations and live in your head." You've got to chuckle over a system that has you watching women for their sexual attractiveness and wants you to experience their sexual attractiveness in your head!

**

STUDENT

When I think about going to the gym, a subtle discomfort starts in my stomach, below the ribcage, all across the front, a slight tension or ache. My unconscious reaction is to do something else, not to go work out. Amazing to observe that I react so automatically to something so subtle with behavior I don't like. I don't even make a conscious meaning connection such as, "Working out will be uncomfortable and unpleasant and I don't want to do it." I just don't work out.

GUIDE

It is amazing, isn't it? We think this is some big, huge, terrifying thing that's motivating us, and in fact it's just unexamined assumptions. But there's nothing in those sensations to stop a workout, is there?

**

It is not possible to maintain an issue without sensations. Without sensations there would be nothing to trigger the emotions, thoughts, labels, beliefs, etc. It is subtle, and we have to be subtler than it is.

STUDENT

As I ponder the process by which I am unable to accept so much of life, I come to the simple conclusion that the degree to which I am unable to accept something is directly proportional to the intensity of the uncomfortable sensations the something evokes, or would evoke if I accepted. True, it is attachment to my beliefs that fuels my inability to accept certain things as they are, but it is ultimately the intensity of the physical feelings that anchors those beliefs and bonds me so strongly to them. I can easily abandon a belief that doesn't serve me at the moment, as long as it does not stir my body in too noticeable a way.

GUIDE

It's easy to feel acceptance when we feel all the right things. When we feel something we're "not supposed to feel," we want to push that feeling away. We try to get away from the unacceptable, and it all gets worse. The energy we use to resist drains us of vitality. When we allow the feelings to be what they are, they pass through.

**

STUDENT

When I feel a pleasant sensation in my genitals, it's like an invitation I can't refuse. So I intensify the sensation, so to speak (alone). Then I worry that this is compulsive, and therefore wrong, because I can't "just say no" once the initial sensation arises. (I also wonder why people bother eating too much food when this feels so much better and is no-cal.) But seriously, this is a long-time problem, and I'd love to either stop worrying about it or stop doing it. I also wonder how, or if, it affects my marriage, but I can't stop the behavior long enough to find out.

GUIDE

In sitting meditation, you are instructed that once the bell rings, you don't move. Even if you have an itch, you're not to scratch it. This is often perceived as irrelevant, inhumane, bizarre. Meditators are encouraged to consider that learning to have an itch that one does not scratch, no matter how urgent, has far-reaching implications for all of life.

You probably know what this is pointing toward. This is an example of "It's not what, it's how." The problem is not the activity *per se*, but the compulsive nature of it. You can't say no. You are without choice. Even though it might be affecting your marriage, you can't conduct an experiment to find out. That's the problem.

So, of course you must conduct the experiment, yes? In the same way the drinker has to not take the drink, the smoker not light that cigarette, the food addict not eat those extra servings, the anorexic must take that bite, the depressed person must move, you have to not follow your conditioning until you see clearly how it does what it does. You must do that because you will not settle for anything less than freedom, right? And that's the right answer for all of us.

I know you were kidding about wondering why people eat too much when your behavior is more fun and calorie-free, but that little jest points at exactly what we're attempting to see in this exploration. Their sensations don't arise in the same place that yours arise. They cannot trade their original sensations for yours any more than you can trade yours for theirs. This understanding is a great source of compassion.

★★

STUDENT

I'm in nonaccepting mode most when I'm in acute pain. Then, the question of acceptance is irrelevant since pain captures the entire field of attention. If I'm uncomfortable in my body, I try avoidance, aversion, seeking relief, complaining, feeling victimized, worrying--in short, everything but acceptance. It's like I forget there's a choice to take a deep breath (in which acceptance just IS), and it doesn't usually occur to me to consciously breathe until I've tried all the others, and they haven't worked, and I'm MORE uncomfortable than when I started.

GUIDE

This is a variation on the old, "When all else fails, read the instructions." Of course, technically, there is nothing in your initial approach that precludes acceptance. I can accept that I'm avoiding, accept that I'm feeling aversion, accept that I'm seeking relief, accept that I'm complaining, accept that I'm feeling victimized, accept that I'm worrying. With awareness practice we learn to bring everything into acceptance, especially those reactions we have to life that we've been taught to find unacceptable. Acceptance includes the whole of our experience.

**

4·THOUGHT

By the time we are ready to observe the mind, most people report that they have a great deal of trouble getting enough distance from the mind to observe it.

You're asked to notice sensations in the body,
and all you get is an onslaught of
judgments, assumptions, labels,
conclusions, beliefs, voices, and stories.

You're asked to observe emotions,
and all you get is an onslaught of
judgments, assumptions, labels,
conclusions, beliefs, voices, and stories.

I hope you can predict what you will get when
you're asked to observe the mind.
That's right: an onslaught of
judgments, assumptions, labels,
conclusions, beliefs, voices, and stories.

Expecting it, we can be prepared.

Let's investigate the mind by looking at the *process* instead of at the *content* (beliefs, stories, opinions, etc.). We can begin by noticing the state of the mind--not focusing on what it is doing, but how it is functioning. In other words, if my issue, the behavior I suffer over, is compulsive cleaning, I notice a sensation like an anthill in my solar plexus. Then I notice the state of my mind. Not the voices, not the self-talk, not the story, but the *quality* of my mind. "My brain feels tight, fast, like it's vibrating. I call it hot brain."

Turning the attention to the process and content of the mind and coming up blank is a standard ploy of egocentric karmic conditioning. When we're in a meditation hall and I ask people to report on the voices in their heads, you could hear a pin drop inside and outside the heads. We go on to something else, and the bedlam in the cranium returns.

Conditioning can lie very low when you start looking. Often I hear people say that as soon as they decide to start meditating, everything in their lives suddenly gets fine. Conditioning says, "I don't want to meditate now, because I'm happy and I'm afraid looking at stuff will be upsetting." Making an agreement not to pursue conditioning so it won't ruin your good time is like making that first payment to a blackmailer.

STUDENT

It seems that the majority of my thoughts are nonaccepting--a constant babble of complaints, critiques, wishes, desires, dislikes, discomforts, stress, fear, etc. It feels like too much to deal with.

GUIDE

It is not necessary to deal with all the content, the issues, of the mind separately. "I'm afraid" has a certain quality in the mind. The stories might be about any of the thousands of things you're afraid of, but the quality of the mind during any of those fears is the same. The "how" of the mind is the same whether you're being beaten up over being a loser or overeating or saying something rude. The state of the mind during beatings is the same regardless of the particulars of the infraction.

It is possible to catch onto the state of mind, regardless of what it is, and disidentify without ever knowing what the content is!

**

EXERCISE

To get a closer look at the quality or the state of the mind during a particular behavior, try this exercise: When you have a few moments during which your conditioning is not torturing you, begin to tell yourself the story surrounding your behavior. Tell the story until conditioning gets "worked up." Watch what happens with the mind. See how the mind does this working up. You will get to see, by doing this volitionally, how it works when you're not doing it volitionally. Jot down your observations.

3·EMOTION

Emotions make things real. If a close friend were to die and you felt nothing, if your job were threatened and you felt nothing, if your partner had an affair and you felt nothing-- for many people this would be a signal that "something's wrong." The level of feeling we have about something tells us how important that thing is to us.

If you look across the breakfast table at your partner and your heart swells with emotion, you know you're having the  right feeling and your relationship is going well. (Not that this is conscious, though it might be.)

If you look across the table and feel anger or resentment, you might conclude that the relationship needs work, possibly professional assistance.

If you look across the table and feel nothing, this is the most significant "feeling" of all. Feeling nothing often is interpreted to mean that this relationship is beyond trouble, it's over.

As long as we're feeling the "right emotion" and feeling it to an appropriate degree, we can feel like the right/appropriate person. All of this is conditioned beliefs and assumptions. I would suggest that far from being true or good or right or beneficial, such conditioned beliefs about emotion are destructive.

STUDENT

When you start talking about emotions, I feel scared at the thought of avoiding/denying my feelings, which is how I interpret what you say. I hear, "Don't have feelings," like they're only sneaky little awful things, so just look at them coolly and don't have much to do with them. And I really have a resistance to that! I feel angry, mad, and cheated.

GUIDE

Remember, I'm just asking folks to consider their beliefs about emotion. This isn't behavior modification or self-improvement. We're watching closely to see what happens. It is my contention, I admit, that what you will see is that the emotions don't mean what you believe they mean and therefore needn't have the power over you that they have. That's not the same as not being allowed to have your emotions. I would just like for you to be clear about what you're having.

**

EXERCISE

When we bring compassionate awareness to our lives and notice the role emotion plays, we see two things: how we feel in a particular situation, and how we feel about how we feel. We quickly catch on that our emotions are not the problem. It's our feelings about our emotions that cause us to suffer.

Continue to observe the issue you chose on page 96.

Notice the conditioning you have about your emotions. Explore not only your emotions, but also how you feel about your emotions.
For example:
1) What would you conclude about yourself if you woke up tomorrow with no feelings about this issue?
2) What would your relationship to this issue be if you had no emotion about it?
3) What is your emotional reaction to others who have the same issue you do?

Write down what you see.

When describing emotions, it can be helpful to
use non-emotional terms such as full, tight,
heavy, constricted, or "like an elephant sitting
on my chest." (These terms describe
sensations.) Also, it is important not to let
describing replace observing. We habitually
look to the conditioned mind for a label and
then feel that our work of paying attention is
over. But a word to describe an emotion is
no more helpful in ending suffering than a
word describing food is satisfying to a hungry
stomach.

STUDENT

I had an insight about a pattern I've noticed.
My head interprets and labels a sensation as
a certain emotion, assigns meaning to the
emotion (already established through
conditioning), then makes up a story.
Sometimes the story is a good one at first,
but usually it isn't long before I'm suffering.
I have found that I can back out of the story
at just about any point (if I wake up and
realize it's a story), right up until it has me
hooked and there is no way out but to go

through it. But part of me gets really afraid and believes I will suffer forever. At this point I usually go to one of my addictions to shut up the story.

GUIDE

I bet you're correct about going to one of the addictions to shut up the story. Then, if you're like most of us, you get another go-round for having indulged an addiction. Have you tried dropping the whole thing and turning your attention to breathing? The story is throbbing along, and you suddenly come to. "Oh, I know where to turn my attention! I'll focus on the breath."

These are the three keys to your success: pay attention, pay attention, and pay attention. As you watch, things will slow down and become spacious. Then you will be able to see clearly all sorts of things that at first seem hidden and mysterious.

**

STUDENT

I have heard you say "First we accept, then we roll up our sleeves." This led to a breakthrough in my understanding of acceptance. In life there is work to be done. Sometimes the work includes pain. When we resist, it's just like the force of friction, and the friction limits the amount of meaningful work we can do. When we accept, we are not giving in; instead we are no longer burning out our energy on friction and we are more able to make a difference in life. What we do may not make the difference we want, but we won't be wasting energy that could become love. Even if we're accepting and there's no friction, we may not be the part that can make the difference. Perhaps through acceptance we can see more clearly and know where to act.

GUIDE

When we're present, the next step is revealed to us. Maybe there is something to do, maybe not. Whether there is action to take or not, being here, in the moment, where the action is, is our best opportunity to provide what life asks for.

⋆⋆

STUDENT

Various emotions are associated with different aspects of my issue--pessimism. When I am in the thick of believing the worst-case scenario, the identifiable emotion is fear. It's almost a full-blown panic, at least for a few seconds. When I think about the role this issue plays in my life, the emotion I experience is anger. I hate that I live with this torture. But underneath, I think what both the fear and anger are trying to avoid are genuine experiences of either joy or sadness. Through all this I am seeing that the route away from suffering, over this or any issue, is to pay attention all the time. I can see it's the only way not to get caught up in the stories and emotions.

GUIDE

Why are we taught to live in fear, controlled by our terror of being out of control, approaching life as inadequate children rather than free adults? Because fearful people are easily controlled. A person who is without fear cannot be controlled.

**

STUDENT

Looking at the emotions connected with my behavior, I see shame, embarrassment, self-disgust. What if I had none of those feelings about this behavior? Immediately a voice pops up: "Then you'd really be crazy. If you didn't feel shame and embarrassment that you sometimes check the front door lock three times in one night, then you'd spend the whole night checking. You need this shame and embarrassment to keep your desire for safety within reasonable bounds, to keep you safe." So, my assumption is that self-loathing keeps me safe... hm. The first sensation that makes me feel I have to stop what I'm doing and check that I'm "safe" is a tingling in my upper chest. That's followed by a shortness of breath and sometimes pressure above and behind my eyebrows.

GUIDE

I would say that self-loathing keeps you
"safely" in the grip of conditioning and safe
from having the life of peace and joy that is
your birthright. How about a little game to
help you out when you're being bamboozled
by conditioning? Take a piece of paper and a
pen with you as you go around the house
closing it up for the night. Make a note of
each thing you've locked. Say to that part of
you who is concerned about making everything
safe, "Good job. Now let's go around one
more time so you feel really sure." Put a
check mark by all the locks you rechecked.
Acknowledge the good work and go to bed.
That way when the voice starts in you can
reassure the frightened part of you that you
know everything is done, and all is okay.

**

STUDENT

I've been feeling strong anxiety in my body.
Last night when I went to bed an episode
began, and I found myself wondering, if I
were not attached emotionally to this

sensation, what would it be like? I noticed immediately that the sensation subsided, and the cascade of thoughts which normally begin to spiral out of control stopped as well. What astounded me was what occurred immediately afterward. My day ran through my mind like a movie, showing me the things that supported fear-filled thought, such as anxiety about work and watching television most of the evening even though I wanted to call family and friends. I saw my childhood and family life as I watched this "movie." I realized I was conditioned to be afraid. This all occurred in just a few minutes, and as I watched, the anxious feeling just melted away.

STUDENT

Emotions carry such importance for me. My story is that emotions are a problem that I have to solve immediately. "Stop everything, I'm having an emotion!" "Fix them!" "Have the right emotions for once in your life, will you?"

STUDENT

I found that I do not really know what emotion means. I looked it up in the dictionary, and of course it said "a feeling," which was not very helpful. It also said "any of various complex reactions with both mental and physical manifestations, such as love, hate, fear, anger, etc." This is interesting; the "mental and physical manifestations" intrigues me. My issue is worry, and the emotion that I have usually felt is fear. When I watch the sensation closely and I watch the story come up and don't believe it, then the emotion does not occur.

GUIDE

We learned to associate strong emotions with specific behaviors, and we haven't stopped to question those associations. Emotion/behavior bonds were learned in childhood and are still running our lives. "But aren't my emotions real and true? Wouldn't I be less than human if I didn't respond as I do?" Well, no. I suggest that if we uncouple those associations and separate the components we can cease suffering over a bunch of unexamined assumptions.

For example, we are conditioned to think that feeling guilty if we disappoint someone we love is one way of knowing we love. To the suggestion that we examine our emotions, we may react by saying, "Do you mean I shouldn't feel guilty if I let down my loved one? What kind of unloving person would I be if I didn't care about the feelings of my beloved? I couldn't really love someone if I didn't care how they feel."

There are a number of unexamined assumptions in that string of thoughts. First, scrutinizing emotions in general and specific emotions in particular is not the same as deciding which emotions are the right ones and which are the wrong ones. Emotions are simply emotions. My point is that most people don't know what emotions are in general and have no idea that emotions are linked to past events and have no information about how and why.

Second, emotions do not mean anything about our character. Feeling fear doesn't mean I'm a bad person. We feel as we feel because we've concluded that's the way we feel and that's just how it is. ("I can't help it. I don't like _____ and never have and that's just how it is.") We make ourselves right in this matter because being right is necessary for survival. Even if I'm a way I shouldn't be emotionally (I'm a crybaby or I have an uncontrollable temper), I know I'm that way, I have good reasons for being that way, I feel bad about it, I'm working on it, and I regularly punish myself for being a way I shouldn't be.

Third, we are frightened when we have a reaction we have been taught we shouldn't have or when we fail to have a reaction we have been taught we should have.

> Our identity is in reacting
> the way we've always reacted.

"This is the kind of person I am. I've always been this way. I can't help it. I've tried to work on this, but I remain pretty much the same." Feeling guilty because you disappoint someone you care about confuses a conditioned reaction with love and misunderstands the nature of both those experiences.

For the record, we don't hurt other people, people hurt themselves. We don't disappoint people, people disappoint themselves. Other people don't make us feel guilty, we feel guilty because we're conditioned to feel guilty. We don't feel guilty because we do something wrong, we feel guilty because we've been taught to feel guilty. We never put anyone's emotional needs before our own. Never. Never. Never.

**

5·BEHAVIOR

Conditioned behavior drives us, through the
suffering it causes, to the need to accept. In
this sequence we are exploring behavior
comes last, but when we attempt to wake up
and see the causes of suffering, we usually
look first to our actions.

Examples of conditioned behavior:
Habits
Routines
Over-eating
Neglecting health
Leaving too soon
Staying too long
Compulsions
breaking commitments
biting nails
daydreaming

Of course, this list is endless.

The deep suffering caused by conditioned behaviors left over from childhood drives us to seek another way of responding to life. When treating ourselves and others unkindly becomes more painful to continue than to stop, we will consider letting go those old survival strategies and opening to possibilities we did not know existed.

An Example

Let's follow sensation-thought-emotion-behavior with this example:

"I have always been overweight. As a child, I was pudgy, and by age eleven I hated my body. I had baby fat into my twenties. I dealt with my body image issues by hiding out and binge-eating. For several years I was bulimic. I've tried every diet known and made up a few on my own. I've probably lost several thousand pounds in my lifetime, ten or twenty pounds at a time, and gained it right back."

What sensations are associated with this issue?
"Tingling in my solar plexus, dryness in my mouth, hollowness in my throat."

For most people, it can be quite difficult at first to locate the sensations in the body, but it's important to develop that level of awareness. At some time a sensation in the body was connected to a traumatic event. In a flash, a connection was made: "I don't ever want to feel that way again. This is bad, wrong, horrible. I must get away, or I won't survive." Of course we weren't consciously aware of having that reaction, coming to that conclusion, or making that decision. We can't recall it today. It would seem that the whole event is buried far down under layers of life experience.

In fact, it is present right now, in every unconscious moment of our lives. It and thousands of reactions like it make up the childhood survival system that I call egocentric karmic conditioning. Each moment that we are operating out of habit rather than conscious, compassionate awareness is a moment in which those five steps of movement, sensation, thought, emotion, and behavior are swirling about dictating our experience of life.

Sitting still and observing minutely enables us to find the exact place in the body where the sensation that is the origin of an entire complex of suffering is held. Once we realize that a sensation does not need to be followed by the thought-emotion-behavior pattern, we are freed up to do the work of dismantling the structure of our suffering.

What thoughts arise about this issue?
"I want to be thin. I don't want to be fat. I want to be like everybody else so I'll be loved. It's not healthy to be fat. I'm so embarrassed by the way I look."

Within the thoughts, you can identify distinct voices. Some will say things like, "You are a fat, disgusting pig. How could anyone ever love you? If you had willpower, if you weren't so lazy, you could take off some of that lard." Other voices will respond, "Oh, go ahead and have something sweet. You've been working really hard, and you deserve it. You're never going to have a relationship; you may as well have something good to eat. No one cares what you look like anyway. What are another few pounds?"

This self-talk--indeed, most self-talk--comes directly from childhood. In adults, it functions to maintain old, no-longer-useful-and-perhaps-never-were-useful structures or habits. In fact, the thoughts themselves are habits. We are afraid not to believe them. We believe they are real and wise and helping us through life. When we bring conscious, compassionate awareness to our self-talk, we can see that its only function is to maintain old patterns by keeping us confused about who we really are. (Hint: We are not those voices.)

What emotions arise in response to these thoughts?
"I feel sad. I feel lost and empty and alone and desperate."

When we react out of habit, egocentric karmic conditioning has us right where it wants us. When self-talk leaves us feeling defeated, we can know that we have given our life over to karma, self-hate, the illusion of separation, childhood conditioning, suffering.

What behaviors follow those emotions?
"I start a new diet. And I continue to overeat."
Behavior catches our attention and goads us to seek another way. Behaviors are deeply ingrained.

Switching one behavior for another
is what we usually believe
will give us the life experience we want,
but that's illusion.

Acceptance of all aspects
of who and how we are
in every moment is the way to have
the life experience we seek.

PART THREE

Acceptance, Freedom,
and Possibility

We Can Wake Up.

Change is difficult. But heroes require great challenges, and this a heroic path. Seeing through this mass of conditioned insanity is really hard. It's hard because

we've been conditioned
to think what's not true,
believe what's absurd,
and be terrified
of the feelings in our bodies.

If seeing through
egocentric karmic conditioning were easy,
we would have done it long ago.

"Every time I have that little twinge-y movement in my body I start thinking about such and such and feeling thus and so and doing this or that. Isn't that silly? Doesn't make any sense. I'll just stop." We haven't stopped though, because we're programmed to be confused and find the whole process mysterious and subtle and unavailable to us.

So, we just keep going through life
as suffering little automatons.

However, our situation is not terminal.
We can wake up.
We can end suffering.
We can let everything go,
know nothing,
and breathe.

Conscious compassionate awareness
enables us to see
where we are
and how we cause ourselves to suffer.

When we accept who and how we are, accept
everything that has resulted in what we are
right now, we can be present with ourselves
in a way that ends the suffering.

STUDENT

To get love, a part of me has always tried to be "the right person." When I love that person inside me who has been working so hard to be the right person, she has what she has always wanted.

GUIDE

Suffering ends when who I am is accepted and embraced in compassion. When I accept myself with compassion, it's clear that how I am is not a problem. My old behaviors were in reaction to beliefs, assumptions, confusion, self-hate, and attempts to reject myself into being the person I thought I should be.

**

Being HERE

Back and forth we go:

Identified with conditioning,
                    returning to center.
The world looks this way,
                    the world looks that way.
I'm miserably suffering,
                    I'm joyfully free.
There's a big problem,
                    everything is just fine.

This path offers us the possibility of living
H·E·R·E
with life as it is, in well-being, no matter what.

Being
H·E·R·E
is more interesting than being anywhere else.

Not just free of suffering, but more fun,
more exciting, more alive. Being still in
awareness (even as our bodies race around)
is bliss.

The Zen Fool

Often, when we're working hard to see what's going on with us, laughter is an indication that we've disidentified, that we've stepped back far enough to get a broader perspective. It's not so much that what we're seeing is funny, it's that the relief of suddenly being free of attachment causes us to laugh spontaneously.

The ultimate "Zen person" is the fool. Why? Because to an egocentric illusion of a separate self, a person not operating from conditioning appears foolish. By the time we have been conditioned into an unnatural enough state to fit into society, authentic being looks silly, childish, unsophisticated, definitely not "cool."

Remember that Jesus said, "You must become as little children." Little children are innocent. They don't have control and don't think they should have. Life is a great big playground and they want to play. When it hurts they cry; when it's fun, they laugh.

Spiritual Liberation Olympics

The quality of your life is determined by the focus of your attention. I do not mean "the glass is half full or half empty." This is not a matter of learning to look on the bright side of life. For example, if I'm a worrier, I can attempt to focus my attention on the "positives" in life and distract myself from worry. But that won't accomplish my desired goal, because while I'm distracting myself from worry, part of my attention must be on the worry I'm trying to avoid. (Just don't think

STOP
I SHOULDN'T WORRYING
WORRY
WORRY IS
USELESS
DON'T
WORRY
WHY
WORRY?

about peanut butter.) If, however, I take the approach of acceptance, I don't need to attempt to avoid, nor must I remain stuck in worry. What I can do is accept that I worry. I'm conditioned to worry. My conditioned behavior says nothing about my inherent goodness and adequacy as a person. Worry is a habit, an emotional response to a thought arising from a sensation triggered by the movement of energy. Nothing more.

My work now is to get to the bottom of this habitual reaction so that my attention, energy, and life force are no longer trapped in relationship to the habit. I see through conditioned patterns of reaction. I accept that I worry. I don't need to take it personally. I can find where the sensations of worry reside in my body. I can watch how those physical feelings are labeled, how the labels are expressed through voices in my head, how the voices are creating and maintaining a story, how I'm conditioned to believe the story and all the story means.

I can watch how emotion arises in reaction to the story the voice is telling me, and how I'm conditioned to behave when in the grip of this sequence of reactions.

This is our practice. This is how we transform
our stumbling, suffering life into the
exhilarating flight of a dive.

At first it's scary, and we find all sorts of
reasons to avoid facing that vast, open space
beyond the familiar constrictions of our
conditioned reactions. But each time we take
the leap and discover that we not only
survive but enjoy a moment of unimagined
freedom, courage grows.

Resistance and aversion will continue to arise.
Meanwhile, the process of looking deeply and
seeing clearly becomes its own reward.
Eventually, we acknowledge that we are in
training--for the Spiritual Liberation Olympics.
As with any training, there is a direct
correlation between what we put into it and
what we achieve.

We've explored the critical sequence of bringing attention to movement sensation, thought, emotion, and behavior. Now let's look at some key components that support us in spiritual practice.

The Breath

Maintaining a steady focus is as important in awareness practice as maintaining good form is for diving. Our primary focus is the breath. Allowing the attention to rest on the breath brings us right into the present moment.

I encourage people to stay with the breath at all times. It's calming in fearful situations, and it just plain old makes life more joyful.

Staying with the breath takes practice. In the beginning, as we attempt to focus on  the breath, attention darts around like a hummingbird in springtime. As we practice, we will begin to feel the breathing as a background of awareness within which all activity arises. This is what is meant by practicing present-moment awareness. Being in the present dissolves the whole chain of conditioned reactions.

Accepting "What Is"

Acceptance is a synonym for being at one with what is. Life accepts. Life is accepting. All life is clearly acceptable to life. Only we human beings resist life as it is.

Until we drop, even for an instant, the illusion of being separate from life, we cannot perceive "what is." We assume that what we perceive is what is, but our perception is conditioned. Our perception is filtered through our beliefs, assumptions, and projections. Only from a disidentified, centered perspective can we see what is as it actually is.

All helpful awareness comes to us via insight, not through the comparisons, judgments, and conclusions of conditioned mind, which does not live in the present. It exists, as an illusion, when we are imagining the past or the future. Conditioned mind has no information for us.

Conditioned emotions have no information for us. A conditioned emotion is a habit. It has nothing to do with what is in this moment. We feel something and look to conditioned mind to tell us what we are feeling. Then we get the same old story about what we feel, who we are and what life is, and we miss the opportunity to be present, to responsively sense the moment in which we are arising. When we are present, we come into existence with the moment.

Energy

One way we can be more responsive to each moment is to become aware of our energy, or what we might call "spirit." What is your energy like generally? Experiment with giving attention to the quality of your energy, how it changes, how it is related to each sensation, thought, emotion sequence. What is it like when you're living in "something wrong" mind, or when you're worrying or depressed? How about when you're disidentified?

In working with people over the years, I've noticed that it is much easier for us to observe other people's energy than our own. The boss walks into the meeting preceded by a cloud of "something's wrong." You walk into the house at the end of the day and sense immediately that there's "trouble" in the house. Before you see your best friend's face, you can feel the "low spirits." You watch the kids come in from their event, and you can know how it went by "reading" their energy. We've probably all had the experience of wanting to leave a place because it just doesn't feel right. Conversely, you can walk into a room and feel at home, as if you could live there forever.

We're often oblivious to our own energy. The reason is that we're looking out through the eyes of the conditioned aspect of ourselves that's running our lives at the moment, the aspect we're identified with. From that perspective, our energy feels appropriate. We may have no idea that someone tuning into our energy will know immediately that we are preoccupied or angry or sad.

We can learn to see energy or spirit in ourselves, for ourselves.
☆ Watch the energy in your body move back and forth between expanded and contracted.
☆ Watch for energy changes in your emotions between "positive" and "negative."
☆ Pay attention to the mind--are frontal lobes relaxed or tight?

☆ Are your thoughts of "something wrong," or are you in "possibility"?

☆ Can you sense how much of your spirit is free to be present and how much is locked up in identification with conditioning?

☆ What happens to your energy when you're here, and what happens to it when you're fantasizing about the future or reviewing the past?

☆ What is your energy like when you're caught up in your story?

EXERCISE

Focus on the issue you chose to work with on page 96, or another behavior you struggle with. What is your energy like when you are caught in that behavior? When you are not caught in it?

Issue
$

When I am scared about $

STUDENT

When I'm taking life personally, my energy
goes to the story or to the other person and
becomes contracted. I'm hyper, afraid,
untrusting, unsafe, frozen, disconnected, and
trying to become invisible. When I'm present,
my energy expands. I'm relaxed, open,
trusting, happy, confident, safe, loving, and
feeling that everything is just fine. I see it
as a matter of choice from moment to
moment. I've been practicing expanding, just
for the fun of it!

STUDENT

Even though it is difficult to identify the
sensations, I am trying to sit with them and
not react to them. I am aware that if I stop
and sit with what I am feeling, I have a shot
at not going into the defensive, egocentric
behavior that would normally follow. My trust
in this process enables me to accept the
uncomfortable space that I would otherwise
have filled with some regrettable action.

GUIDE

Sometimes the quickest way to see what's going on is to stop the conditioned behavior. This often causes the system to intensify the sensations to keep the cycle going. For example, if I'm a smoker and I want to find the sensations that mean "have a cigarette," deciding not to smoke for a while will probably heighten the sensations that precipitate the behavior.

**

STUDENT

All around me, inside and out, is endless sensation and motion. Sometimes it feels pleasant. When it feels pleasant, I hope it won't change. It always changes. Sometimes it feels unpleasant. When it feels unpleasant, I hope it will change. It always changes. Watching it--more accurately, watching all the many "its"--that is all there is, endless "its." Sometimes pleasant, sometimes unpleasant. On it goes...

GUIDE

And on "you" can go, allowing awareness to expand far beyond the current "it."

✶✶

STUDENT

What I notice when I catch myself chewing on or picking at my fingers (my issue) is that my mind is on auto-chatter. I am often not doing anything but sitting, but my mind is working like a buzz-saw. I also notice there are layers to the mind noise. Some things are 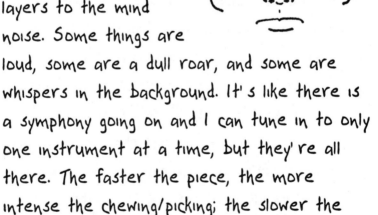 loud, some are a dull roar, and some are whispers in the background. It's like there is a symphony going on and I can tune in to only one instrument at a time, but they're all there. The faster the piece, the more intense the chewing/picking; the slower the piece, the less intense the behavior.

   This is fascinating to me. I have never really paid attention to this. If I was present all the time and not on auto-chatter, would my behavior just cease? Is it possible to be present 24/7?

GUIDE

It is absolutely possible to be present 24/7. However, for most folks being present 3/7 or 4/7 would change life from miserable to joyful. That's why we encourage sitting in meditation for a few minutes every day. The more you're present, the better you feel, and the better you feel, the more you want to be present.

     We are programmed to leave the present in times of intensity. When we encounter frightening, stressful, upsetting life circumstances, we are programmed to go unconscious and act out of survival strategies. When we attempt to stay conscious, the programming escalates. But conditioning can maintain this barrage of fear stories and predictions of doom for only so long. We are programmed to buckle before it does, so our work is to hang in there longer than it can. When we do that, we get to see how it operates and how it affects us. We see what is behind it and the belief systems holding it in place. Watching is the key.

Out in the middle of our watching, we can run into what is called in Zen "going farther and faring worse." The more we see, the worse it looks. Conditioning escalates, the voices grow louder, the stories are more terrifying, and all we want to do is run back to the "safety" of doing what conditioning tells us to do.

What is the way out?
Turn the fall into a dive.

Accept. Breathe. Don't argue, don't fight, don't resist. Just breathe. Just notice. Give up any ideas about getting anywhere. Peaceful, nonviolent sit-ins will accomplish everything we want to accomplish. Just sitting and breathing and noticing.

Regardless of what might be happening, if you bring all your attention and awareness to the breath, not only will you be just fine, you will see everything you need to see.

**

Practice

We come back to the moment over and over--that's why we call this practice. We return again and again until being here becomes not second nature, but what it truly is, first nature. Letting go of the conditioned thoughts, voices, stories, meanings, and habits becomes easy. Being here becomes easy. We learn that we can simply stay still, allowing sensations to be sensations rather than the prelude to a sixteen-act play we've seen a bazillion times.

We are not creating a system or formula for enlightenment here.

> We are learning to see things
> as they are,
> rather than as we have been
> conditioned to believe they are.

My jaw tightens, there's a knot in my solar plexus, and my hands clench. I don't need to believe this means 1) I'm angry, 2) I need to

be angry, 3) I have to hit somebody, 4) I'm a bad person, 5) I should do something about myself, or anything else. These are conditioned associations. Period. I can see them for what they are, I can see through them, and I can be free to do or not do anything.

Remember, all these arise simultaneously and are not random. When I'm caught in a particular story, my mind feels a certain way, my emotions feel a certain way, and the sensations in my body feel a certain way. It is a standard program. They all arise together, the same way every time.

I ask people to find the initial sensations in the body and stay with those feelings because, without a deep awareness practice, people cannot watch a story without getting caught up in it. When we can stay with the feelings in the body, we can see that those feelings don't mean that story. They're just sensations. The story is the story, and it is out there floating around in karma-land. Stay with the bodily sensations, and there is nothing supporting the story. With nothing supporting it, the story loses its power to captivate and enthrall. After a while it starts sounding silly. ("They are judging me and want me to go away because there's something wrong with me, and...") When it arises, we don't believe it. In that moment we taste freedom.

The World of Opposites

When following the sequence of movement, sensation, thought, emotion, and behavior, you will quickly notice that there's not one story but two. There's not one voice speaking to you, there are two voices and they're expressing opposite perspectives. I call this process the duality slide. The duality slide maintains the world of opposites, the land of comparison that makes suffering instantly and constantly available. For instance, in the example of the worrier, one story is about how I should worry because there is so much to worry about, while the other story is about the absurdity of worrying. One voice is devoted to terrifying me with everything that could go wrong, while the other harangues me for indulging in a wrong, stupid, loser activity such as worrying. (For a more complete discussion of this phenomenon please refer to our book *Be the Person You Want to Find.*)

EXERCISE

---See what happens to your body when you accept and when you resist. Where do you tense/relax/hold/feel pain, etc.?

---Notice thoughts accompanying acceptance and resistance. Is acceptance a thought, or is it something that just happens and is therefore not noticed? Is resistance a thought, or is it something that just happens and is therefore not noticed? What roles do activities like repeating thought patterns or depressing thoughts play? See if you can be aware of what takes up the space in your thinking process.

---Look to see what happens with you emotionally when you accept and when you resist. What happens when you feel strong emotion around either of these?

EXTRA CREDIT ASSIGNMENT

See if you can observe all this through a filter of acceptance. In other words, see if you can accept that you resist.

If you can accept that you resist,
you will be able to observe the resistance.

If you resist your resistance,
you won't be able to see how you resist.

STUDENT

The first sensation is fluttering at the top of my abdomen. Associated with it is a feeling in my arms like adrenaline being released. I've gotten familiar enough with it that I recognize it several times a day, but I still can't stop my emotions from taking a nosedive. I am trying to notice my emotions without thinking the same things I always think, but it is very hard. I have also discovered that the fluttery feeling leads to all kinds of crummy emotions and not just to the one I was initially looking at. I find that interesting.

GUIDE

What we're required to do is find willingness and courage not to go with the pull of conditioning. As you practice you'll begin to watch those emotions take a nosedive and recognize you are not the emotions or the nosedive. "You" are the awareness observing them.

★★

STUDENT

I am newly aware of the contents of my mind. I am understanding just how tiny this "mind" I have used to run my life is, and in a way it is scary. In another way it is a relief to realize how misleading it is to believe what goes on in my mind. I have allowed beatings to occur because I "should" have known how to do something, or I "should" have had the right answers. It makes me laugh that this mind is so sure it is right, when it is so impossible for it to be right. It couldn't possibly know everything! How sad and stuck it is. As I pay attention I realize just how powerful my belief in it has been. It has shaped my entire world.

GUIDE

We choose our beliefs over our experience. The survival system keeping our reality in place is based on beliefs. We project our beliefs onto life. We see our projections and believe we are seeing life. Until we find the courage to look beyond our beliefs, we will live life inside our own projections, believing we are living in life as life is. Until we find the willingness to accept what is, we will not have the courage to go beyond our beliefs. We say, "That makes me uncomfortable," and believe discomfort is reason enough to leave, to reject, or to withdraw. Can you imagine what your life would be like if discomfort were irrelevant?

"I'm afraid." "I feel anxious." "I'm nervous." "It's scary." For most people those simple sentences translate into, "Something's wrong/I don't want this/goodbye." What might happen if you sat still through the series of sensations labeled "fear" and proved to yourself that those sensations don't mean anything? What if you approached the sensations labeled nervous or anxious or scary as a call to attention rather than as a danger signal that means "I'm outta here!"? "Ah, what's this? Is there anything here that needs attention? Let me stop what I'm doing and pay attention to how I'm feeling."

The body is a receiving station. We are constantly receiving signals from everything around us. It is helpful to be present to what

is happening in our vicinity. There might, in
fact, be something that requires our
immediate response. If there is, it is well
that we are present to respond. If there is
not, it is to our advantage not to leapfrog
our way along a conditioned string of
associations leading to hell.

Conscious, compassionate awareness
makes all the difference, doesn't it? When
you're there with you, with yourself, accepting
yourself as you are, there's no problem.
Nothing to fix.

**

STUDENT

I am a mental health therapist, so my
training and orientation has always focused on
change. The title of your book *There's
Nothing Wrong With You* intrigued me because
it seems as if there *is* something wrong, or
at least something that one could do better.
After reading more of your books, I've
changed my thinking as a therapist. Now I
work on getting clients to accept themselves
exactly as they are, because therein lie the

seeds of change. I still laugh at the irony--
once you accept yourself, old behaviors just
drop away. When you try to force yourself to
change, you get nowhere.

STUDENT

Since starting awareness practice and learning
to focus attention the way you suggest, I've
been working with my behavior of repeatedly
checking doors at night, and my compulsion has
lessened. At the same time, though, I've
spun into a panic in another area of my life.
I might have gotten nervous and panicky
about this other area anyway, but I wonder if
this hysteria is conditioning rearing its head,
showing it doesn't want to let go.

GUIDE

Oh, I think we can count on conditioning
rearing its head anytime you attempt to do
something threatening to ego maintenance.
Our conditioning is a survival system. It is
designed to keep the identity intact regardless
of the source of the challenge. Conditioning is
not going to be any more receptive to your

better ideas about how you should be different than it is to other people's ideas about how you could "improve" yourself. If you decide you want to be conscious, conditioning will fight you tooth and nail to maintain control over your life.

The good news is you're practicing a process for dealing with it. You're learning to see how fear is created in you. You're learning to disidentify from what you've been taught to believe so that you can be present to what is. You're seeing how you can be with yourself in a compassionate way while all this misery is being generated.

It's actually simpler than it appears. The suffering is all the same process, and we go beyond it in the same way every time. When you panic, you have the same set of "symptoms" every time. It is very helpful when we can see that what we're up against is not a bunch of complex, complicated, intricate unknowns we must dissect and figure out, but rather one big package of programming. It is way easier to step back and realize "I am not that."

Equally helpful is that once we see through one issue, we can apply this same process to our next area of suffering.

**

STUDENT

I don't accept being human. I don't accept that my mind is the way it is, and that I can't trust my own thoughts. I don't accept that karma affects my life. I don't believe there are different aspects to my personality or, that I can't figure out the answer. Deep down I believe there is a right and good way to be, that there are lots of problems to solve, and that all the debates in my head will get me somewhere. I truly want to know what I am, why I am here, and where we all came from. I want to know the meaning of it all. Somewhere deep down I cannot let these things go.

Conditioning is telling me that awareness practice is too much work and that it might be better if I gave it up. I could go back to drinking and my other distractions. Funny how it idealizes the things I used to do.

The part it forgets is how happy I am now. It seems that I need to accept these deeply buried nonacceptances and beliefs. The resistance is quite strong and relentless and, right at this moment, seems like Mt. Everest.

GUIDE

I love it when our process is laid out this clearly. All this thrill-of-victory, agony-of-defeat drama is not a lot of fun, but to see the conditioning, sentence by sentence, takes the power away from it.

I often think the best approach to Mt. Everest is a vacation on a white beach, far, far away. If a vacation far away isn't available right now, you could always try the meditator's vacation: some quality time gazing at a blank white wall.

✳✳

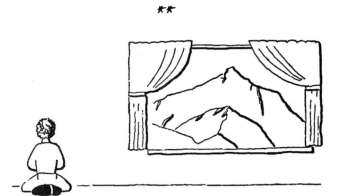

Stay Awake

Conscious compassionate awareness, essential nature, authenticity, presence, never gets tired of being aware, of paying attention. Only egocentric karmic conditioning gets tired of paying attention. This is extremely important. You start paying attention to ego identity, seeing how it works, gaining some distance from it, and it starts whining about being tired! So, until you learn not to believe it, you fall for it, and while you're not paying attention, it rests and rejuvenates. If you don't let it dupe you into going unconscious, if you keep scrutinizing it, it becomes more exhausted. But then it whines, complains, wheedles, and angles again. Once more you think it is you, and you cave in, giving it what it wants. "Oh, I deserve to veg out in front of the tv because I've had such a hard day."

DON'T FALL FOR IT!
STAY AWAKE!
IF YOU WANT YOUR LIFE, STAY AWAKE!

The Compassionate Mentor

To undertake this path, we each need acceptance, care, understanding, unconditional love, compassion, encouragement, a fun companion, a loving parent, a cheerleader, an advocate, a mentor. You can provide all that for a very deserving human being--yourself. Could a life be devoted to anything more important? I doubt it.

Being a loving parent does not mean we sit in the back seat while the kids race around with the car. Being a loving parent means we are always at the wheel, driving as carefully and skillfully as we can, doing our best to keep everyone safe while realizing we have no control. That is also how we mentor ourselves.

When I'm with myself, accepting my conditioned thoughts--not believing them or acting out of them, but accepting them--when I am accepting my emotions and realizing human beings have energy that passes through the body stirring up all sorts of sensations and feelings, I am free to be present, responding to life as it unfolds rather than reacting to old beliefs, fears, and unexamined assumptions.

Where do we get the energy for the life we know in the deepest part of our being is our birthright? We get that energy from doing the work of clearing away all the detritus of our conditioned lives! How do we do that? We sit down, stay still, pay attention to everything, believe nothing, take nothing personally, and we breathe. Here is a summary of the process we have been working with:

1) Recognize that your issue is a conditioned reaction. This is not "you." Remind yourself, "This is not my authentic self; this is a socially conditioned reaction."

2) Practice being present when conditioned reactions arise, and instead of believing what conditioned mind tells you turn your attention to the breath.

3) Notice what is occurring in the body (sensations), the mind (thoughts, voices, and stories), and the emotions.

4) Continue to focus on the breath as you watch the conditioned reactions build up and pass away.

It can be helpful to remind yourself, "My authentic nature is conscious, compassionate awareness." As a focus for the attention, you might repeat to yourself the following:

As I breathe in, I am with the breath.
As I breathe out, I am with the breath.
May all beings be free.
As I breathe in, I'm with the breath.
As I breathe out, I'm with the breath.
May all beings find peace.
As I breathe in, I am with the breath.
As I breathe out, I am with the breath.
May all beings end suffering.
As I breathe in, I am with the breath.
As I breathe out, I am with the breath.
May all beings be happy.

A good definition of mentoring is "compassionately pushing the edges." Often, the best way to know we're on track is to realize we are uncertain. Egocentric, karmic conditioning is very sure about everything. We get fooled because one of the things it is most certain about is how scary and uncertain life is, and how we need to do, feel, and think exactly what it says to survive. It is good to be prepared for all the reactions that are likely to arise when we move beyond our comfort zone and challenge conditioning's authority.

STUDENT

My inability to accept seems to be fear-based. I have realized that nonacceptance feels like protection. But no matter what I do, I expect the pain to be unbearable. If I accept, it will hurt, and if I don't accept, it will hurt, and I've done a lot of hurting already.

Having said all this, I take a deep breath and actually feel better. Maybe I just need to accept that I am stuck and gently embrace the scared child I was and the scared adult I am.

GUIDE

Your last sentence captures our focus perfectly, if we omit "I just need to accept that I am stuck" and cut right to "gently embrace the scared child I was and the scared adult I am." In the moment of embrace, you move from that which is in need of healing to that which heals. We do this moment by moment. All kinds of stuff happened "back then." All kinds of things might happen "out there." True. Right now, gentle embrace. Each moment, gentle embrace. Freedom.

If I want acceptance, I have to accept. If I want love, I have to love. If I want peace, I have to be peace. If I "can't," I can watch carefully to see how and why, and I will know why others "can't." The secret? We get what we do. If I am accepting, I feel accepted. If I am unconditionally loving, I feel unconditional love. If I am peaceful, I live in peace.

⁕⁕

Steps to Success

As your own mentor, here are some things you can offer yourself on this journey.

1) Lower your expectations. Hear what the voices say you should do, then cut those demands by half, then halve them again. It is always wise to do more than conditioning says you can and far less than it says you should.

2) Learn to see "who is here." Cultivate a habit of watching yourself "out of the corner of your eye." When you get information from inside about who you should be and what you should do, ask yourself, "Who says so?" When you find yourself believing something about who you are, ask, "How do I know that?"

3) Create a mini-workbook for yourself by printing the questions below with plenty of space following each one, making copies, and filling them in whenever you have the opportunity. Especially make the effort to

answer the questions when you are caught in conditioning.

--Which aspect of the personality am I identifying with?
--What are the voices saying?
--What is the story I'm believing?
--What kind of reality am I projecting?
--How does my body feel?
--Which emotion am I feeling?
--Is this familiar?
--What happens when I come back to the breath?
--What do I get out of continuing this pattern?

4) Prove to yourself that the fact that life is not easy does not mean you are doing something wrong. Life is hard for conditioned humans because we want life to be other than it is. As we begin to wake up to our conditioning, life can feel even harder because we're beginning to see clearly the disparity between what we've been taught to believe and what is actually so.

5) See for yourself that comparing leads to nothing except more comparing and to suffering. Comparing myself to others who are "better" (I'm a loser) or are "worse" (I'm right, they're wrong) gets me nowhere except stuck and miserable.

6) Don't quit. When we're meditating, we count the breath from one to ten. If we get distracted, go to sleep, or lose consciousness, we begin our counting again at one. We don't say, "Oh, this is too hard. I'm not good at this. I'd better quit." (Okay, sometimes we do, but we know that's not the right answer!) We realize waking up is difficult, we recommit to our effort, and we begin counting again at one. Patiently, humbly, willingly we begin again at one. When we do our best and don't meet the standards of conditioning, we see the standards for what they are (designed to ensure failure), drop the standards, and begin again at the beginning. Quitting is not on our list of options.

7) Learn to see life as an opportunity, not as a problem. Remember that what we're doing is

waking up and ending suffering. This is not meant to be a process that causes suffering!

8) Find other folks who are making a similar effort to wake up. Find time every day for silence, solitude, and sitting. Make conscious efforts every day to spend more time in yes than in no.

Blanket of Acceptance

Consciously seeking out resistance in sensations, thoughts, and emotions is acceptance. The acceptance is an embrace. The embrace is like wrapping all of it in a comforter. The content becomes irrelevant as the acceptance flows over and through the entire being.

Here is a guided imagery. If you would like, read it, or ask a friend to read it, into a tape or CD recorder. Leave a few seconds of silence after commas and between sentences.

Sit or lie back and close your eyes.

Turn your attention to your breath, being
with the breath as it enters your body, fills
your body, and then leaves your body.

See if you can let go of everything else,
bringing all your attention and awareness to
your breathing, feeling the body expand with
the inhalation and contract with the
exhalation, seeing if you can breathe all the
air out before you take the next breath in.

Still keeping your attention on your breathing,
see if you can expand your awareness to
include your whole body, feeling whatever
you're resting against, each breath allowing
you to let go and sink back into whatever is
supporting you, feeling your heart beat,
noticing your pulse in various parts of your
body, checking in with your digestion, noticing if
there are any places of tightness or tension
in your body.

If you find tightness or tension, breathe your next inhalation to that part of the body, and as you exhale let the tightness or tension leave your body with the breath.

If there is some way you'd like to move or adjust your physical posture to allow yourself to be more comfortable, do that now.
Now, take another long, deep breath, staying with the breath the whole way, feeling the body expand.

As you release the breath, feel the body contract.

Expand your awareness once again, this time to your emotions, just noticing what you're feeling, noticing where you look to notice what emotion you're feeling.

What emotion would be the opposite of the one you're feeling now? How would you label that opposite emotion? Can you let yourself feel that emotion in your body?

Now take another nice, long deep breath, staying with the breath, allowing your attention and awareness on the breath to help you let go any other concerns.

Expand your awareness once again, this time to your mind, still attending to your breathing, noticing your body rising and falling with each breath.

Become aware of your mind, aware of what is going on in your mind, both the process and the content.

First, be aware of the state your mind is in, the process. How would you describe the state of your mind? Is it settled and calm, busy and agitated, scattered, focused?

And now, how about the content of your mind? Is your mind thinking, planning, creating, escaping, obsessing, worrying? What has occupied your mind?

Take another long, deep breath as you let all that go, and for the next few moments please imagine the softest, warmest, most beautiful, most luxurious comforter in existence. Give yourself a moment to picture that comforter, noticing what it feels like, what it looks like, its texture, its color. Perhaps there's a pattern or design. Notice its thickness, its shape. Keep in mind this is your comforter, and you can make it look and feel any way you choose.

When you have created what is for you right now the perfect comforter, please wrap yourself in its soft, warm, luxurious embrace. As you settle in, allow yourself to realize this comforter is the comforter of acceptance, and when you are wrapped in it you are embraced in perfect, complete, absolute and utter acceptance.

As you breathe in, breathe in the acceptance.

As you breathe out, realize you are both breathing acceptance into the world, adding more acceptance to the world, and making more room inside yourself for more acceptance.

Breathe yourself completely full of acceptance, to the top of your head, to the tips of your toes, and the tips of your fingers. You are completely filled with, surrounded by, and embraced in acceptance. Your whole world is acceptance.

To complete that image of your whole world being acceptance, being embraced by acceptance, consider for a moment anything about yourself, anything in your world, that you have been keeping outside the embrace of acceptance, and consider if you might like to bring that inside your comforter of acceptance so that it too can experience full acceptance, so it too can know the transformative nature of acceptance.

When you're ready, open that comforter
enough to allow in any and everything about
yourself that you have kept in the realm of
"unacceptable." One at a time, bring them in
and surround them with acceptance.

Stay with the breath, breathing in the
acceptance. As you breathe out, make more
room for compassion, for understanding,
more room for even more acceptance.
If there's something that, right now, you feel
you cannot bring into acceptance, see if you
can bring your inability to accept into the
comforter of acceptance. See if you can
accept the part of you who wants to resist
complete acceptance. Just draw that part of
you into the comforter and accept it as well.

Just breathing... relaxing...letting
go...receiving...

As you relax, feel the pleasure of simply
breathing. Allow yourself to be aware of the
power of acceptance, of the transformative,
expansive, quality of acceptance. See if you

are willing to consider that anything can be embraced into acceptance, and that in that embrace, whatever struggles, whatever suffers, whatever experiences itself as unacceptable, unworthy, ugly, or wrong can be, through the power of acceptance, freed to return to its authentic nature, freed to be its full potential for goodness, for compassion.

Resting there, relaxing completely, within the embrace of compassion, just breathing, no tension, no resistance, peaceful, comfortable, at ease. Rejuvenating, revitalizing, empowering, strengthening, acceptance...

Just stay there for as long as you would like, allowing yourself to receive, allowing yourself to be transformed, to be healed, to be comforted, to be soothed.

When you're ready, once again turn all of your attention, all of your awareness, to your breath. Feel the breath deepen in your body, and as the breath deepens in your body, once

again become aware of your body resting
against whatever is supporting it.
Stretch your body just a little, wiggle your
toes, wiggle your finger-tips, wiggle your lips,
bringing all your attention and awareness to
the body, to the breath, and when it feels
like you're as ready as you can be, slowly
open your eyes...

(end of guided imagery)

Often, at this point, conditioning is waiting to bring you back into its world of "safety," which is in fact suffering. But it can't make you not know what you know. It can't make you forget that acceptance, being present and breathing are available for you once you've had that experience. So, you'll get pulled off, distracted, and it will get you back into old unconscious ways, and then you'll wake up. And, if you wake up into compassion, it won't matter that you've been away, only that you're home now.

Breathe. Rest in the present. You never have known what was going to happen or how something would turn out, and you still don't. Nothing has changed. You might remind yourself that even though you never knew, you are fine.

Here's our choice: enjoy life or don't enjoy life. You know you have no control, you know there are no guarantees, you know you are going to die sometime, you know you're going to leave it all behind when you go. Enjoy life, don't enjoy life--the choice is yours.

Acceptance doesn't change anything. Awareness doesn't change anything. And we will never get anything out of being present. As far as I can tell, all we get out of acceptance, awareness and being present is great happiness that life is the way it is, that it is possible to end suffering, and that we can choose to make the movement from suffering to the present time and time again.

We often idealize waking up and not needing to practice conscious compassionate awareness anymore. But that's conditioned mind trying to dupe us again. Why would we want to stop practicing compassionate acceptance of ourselves and our lives?

Practicing compassionate acceptance
is like being in love
and seeing the face of the beloved
in every moment
as if for the first time.

Why would we ever idealize becoming accustomed to or casual about the face of the beloved? To be in awe, in delight, in love every moment for the rest of your life—could anything be better than that? Could there be a greater blessing?

For a current schedule of workshops and retreats, contact us in one of the following ways:

Website: www.thezencenter.org

Email: information@thezencenter.org

Zen Monastery Practice Center
P.O. Box 1979
Murphys, CA 95247

Telephone: 209-728-0860

Fax: 209-728-0861

For a one-year subscription to the Center's quarterly newsletter and calendar of events, *In Our Practice*, send a check for $12.00 along with your name and address.

There Is Nothing Wrong With You
An Extraordinary Eight-Day Retreat
based on the book
There Is Nothing Wrong With You: Going Beyond Self-Hate
by Cheri Huber

Inside each of us is a "persistent voice of discontent." It is constantly critical of life, the world, and almost everything we say and do. As children, in order to survive, we learned to listen to this voice and believe what it says.

This retreat, held at the beautiful Zen Monastery Practice Center near Murphys, California, in the western foothills of the Sierra Nevada, is eight days of looking directly at how we have been rejecting and punishing ourselves and discovering how to let that go. Through a variety of exercises and periods of group processing, participants will gain a clearer perspective on how they live their lives and on how to find compassion for themselves and others.

This work is challenging, joyous, fulfilling, scary, courageous, demanding, freeing, loving, kind, and compassionate—compassionate toward yourself and everyone you will ever know.

For information on attending, contact:
Zen Monastery Practice Center
P.O. Box 1979
Murphys, CA 95247
Ph.: 209-728-0860
Fax: 209-728-0861
Email: information@thezencenter.org

BOOKS FROM CHERI HUBER

Published by Keep It Simple Books & Zen Meditation Center
All titles are available through your local bookstore.

To order call 800-337-3040 to use Visa/MC, Discover.

Mail orders use this form or a separate sheet of paper. Fax orders: 209-728-0861. Send e-mail orders to keepitsimple@thezencenter.org. Request a complete catalog of products. Visit www.thezencenter.org.

___ There Is Nothing Wrong With You*	0-9710309-0-1	$12.00
___ There Is Nothing Wrong With You for TEENS	0-9636255-1-X	$12.00
___ How You Do Anything Is How You Do Everything: A Workbook	0-9636255-5-1	$10.00
___ The Depression Book*	0-9636255-6-X	$12.00
___ The Fear Book*	0-9636255-1-9	$10.00
___ Be the Person You Want to Find*	0-9636255-2-7	$12.00
___ The Key… Is Willingness*	0-9636255-4-3	$10.00
___ Nothing Happens Next	0-9636255-3-5	$8.00
___ Sex and Money: A Guided Journal	0-9636255-7-9	$12.00
___ Suffering Is Optional	0-9636255-8-6	$12.00
___ That Which You Are Seeking Is Causing You to Seek*	0-9614754-6-3	$10.00
___ Time-Out for Parents*	0-9614754-4-7	$12.00
___ The Monastery Cookbook	0-9614754-7-1	$16.00
___ When You're Falling, Dive	0-9710309-1-X	$12.00

Books and tapes are also sold in discounted sets.

Name _____

Address _____

City_____ State_____ Zip_____

Please send the books I have checked above.

I am enclosing $_____

Postage and handling** $_____

7.25% Sales tax (CA only) $_____

Total amount enclosed $_____

* Also available on audiotape.
**Add $3 shipping for the first book and $1 shipping for each additional book.
Send payment (US funds) or Visa, Mastercard, or Discover number to:
Keep It Simple, POBox 1979, Murphys, CA 95247
Orders out of U.S. send double postage. Overpayments will be refunded.